Praise f
SEE ME FOR V

Brian Castner, author of *The Long Walk*

"If you are a military veteran like me, you may find comfort in the familiar as you read. You know these men and women. You know their words and speech patterns, how they tell a story, it all feels right. But other readers will want more, and for good reason. We can't help but hope—though none say so—that producing this volume proved a salve for the men and women contained within it."

Phil Zabriskie, author of *The Kill Switch*

"'I want you guys to understand' begins the first piece in this valuable, powerful collection. What follows are blunt, plain spoken, tales and remembrances that are at once poignant and harrowing and funny and proud and remorseful—and that, yes, will help us understand much more of what these young men and women have seen, been through, survived, and carry with them still."

William Corley, Veteran of Operation Enduring Freedom, PhD

"This visionary collection scores a direct hit on the stereo-types—'heroes or victims or monsters'—that insulate most civilians from the veterans in their midst, and will be a welcome companion both for veterans who have endured the stifling imposition of simplified views of military service and for civilians looking for better opening lines than, 'Did you kill anyone?' or 'Thank you for your service.'"

Matt Gallagher, author of *Youngblood*

"Chronicles of battle are nearly as old as combat itself, but they've taken on a distinct significance in 21st-century America, where war is something we bring to other places, other cultures, other people. That such a thing is being carried out in an entire citizenry's name by a small selection of that citizenry remains a preeminent element of these wars, and our time and place in American history. The gap today between civilian and veteran is pronounced and vast. But is it unbridgeable? It is not. See Me for Who I Am *is for anyone who's ever wondered, 'What was it like?' These twenty talented vet-writers answer that question with directness and courage. I can't wait to see what they write next."*

David J. Danelo, Veteran of Operation Iraqi Freedom, author of *The Return: A Field Manual for Life after Combat*

"This is as authentic as it gets. These essays reflect the eloquent, powerful voice of the 21st-century American combat veterans' collective efforts to navigate their way back into a society that offers gratitude and respect, but lacks empathy and understanding."

Chris Dumaine Leche, PhD, editor of *Outside the Wire: American Voices from Afghanistan*

"The veteran-writers in this collection invite you to witness the most spiritually transformative and physically visceral moments of their lives. The inspired writings of the men and women whose work appears here must be read as a reminder of the many heroes among us who have traded home for the battlefield in order to protect us all."

See Me for Who I Am

See Me for Who I Am

STUDENT VETERANS' STORIES OF WAR AND COMING HOME

Edited By David Chrisinger

Foreword by Brian Castner,
author of *The Long Walk*

Afterword by Matthew Hefti,
author of *A Hard and Heavy Thing*

Cover Design: Phil Pascuzzo
Interior Design: Melissa Mykal Batalin

ISBN 978-1-944079-01-7
LCCN 2015954421

To the men and women
who never got a chance
to tell their stories.

"Tell the truth. Tell the truth with your whole body. Don't spare the reader. You tell it. We killed plenty of people. I mean me. Me. Me. Tell the terror and the horror of it. The total waste of it. Put the truth in your reader's hands. Write a letter. Tell the truth to a real person here in front of you. She wants to hear your story. Tell it to her. I want to hear your story. Tell it to me."

—Larry Heinemann,
Vietnam Veteran and author

CONTENTS

FOREWORD

By Brian Castner

Perhaps no self-contained diorama better represents the modern gulf between our military veterans and average citizens as this set of essays produced in David Chrisinger's remarkable freshman seminar at the University of Wisconsin-Stevens Point.

Freshman seminar. At most colleges and in most classrooms this unthreatening required course has evolved into a crossover ritual mixed with an eclectic reading list. Professors teach about what it means to be a college student, how to write, how to meet homework and paper deadlines. Some try to throw in a bit of required reading vis-à-vis their pet projects, but often there are equal doses of basic life skills, such as instructions on how to do laundry. In sum, it is a symbol of delayed adulthood in modern America.

All of which places Chrisinger's recent freshman seminar, tailored to veterans of Iraq and Afghanistan, in even starker relief. Student Aaron Lewis needs no help learning to operate a washing machine. Instead, in his bridge class he grappled with the fundamental paradox of military service: balancing what he learned in war with what was taken away. After calmly laying out his reasons for attempting suicide following his deployment to Iraq, Lewis somehow still writes about his time in the Army overall, "I like to think that I came out with more than I went in with."

There lies, exposed, that divergent worldview and accumulation of experiences often referred to as the civilian-military divide. When a twenty-two-year-old Afghan War veteran sits next to an eighteen-year-old true freshman, what do they even talk about?

It is a question often on the mind of Chrisinger's students, and they discuss it in this book in straightforward and unadorned prose that barely registers a hint of embarrassment or self-consciousness. How did I end up here? After seeing and doing so much, what have I become?

The answers can be both heartbreaking and therapeutic. As a group, these soldiers-turned-students could be ripped off a recruiting poster: star football players, wrestlers, farm kids, screwups done good by the discipline of military service. Most were infantry grunts or engineers, searching for hidden IEDs. There is no gloss here, and not all of their insights are becoming; some wear a sense of superiority on their sleeve. But such bravado is at least well-earned, and honest. *Here are my warts,* they say, *where are yours?*

With insight and clarity, they display a genuine curiosity in the examination of their new circumstances. Why do they crave work outdoors, mucking stables, raising chickens and goats? Why is it so hard to sit in a classroom? What is it about a manual, repetitive task that brings so much peace? As they remember the grinding but stable routine of dangerous night patrols, the joy of operating the MK19 grenade launcher, the satisfaction of knowing their place in the world, they lay out all the dots for us to see, even if they aren't yet able to connect all of them on their own.

If you are a military veteran like me, you may find comfort in the familiar as you read. You know these men and women. You know their words and speech patterns, how they tell a story—it all feels right. But other readers will want more, and for good reason. They will want answers that cannot be found here, updates, assurance that everything is turning out okay for these men and women as they transition from warrior to student. Chrisinger taught no explicit writing-as-therapy course; but as readers, we can't help but hope—though none say so—that producing this volume proved a salve for the men and women whose writing is contained within it.

Other readers will want to go a step further, though. They will shout at the pages, *Should not this entire exercise be a cautionary tale? Stop,* these readers will say. *Do not join up. Look at what has happened to your potential comrades! Ignore the recruiting poster that bears your likeness! This military life is not what you think!*

In these pages, Ryan Callahan has already provided a response. For thousands of years, from Homer to Hemingway, war stories have both glorified and warned. Callahan read and heard it all.

"I didn't listen though," he writes. *"Young men rarely do."*

Brian Castner
March 4, 2015
Grand Island, New York

INTRODUCTION

By David Chrisinger

During the fall and spring of the 2014-15 school year, I taught a freshman seminar at the University of Wisconsin-Stevens Point for student veterans in which we studied the history of American veterans coming home from war. My hope was that by studying the experiences of those who came before them, my students would gain valuable perspective and would be able to better process their own experiences. One of the many lessons we learned was that regardless of whether a military service member serves in a war zone or not, transitioning from the military to civilian life can be an extremely alienating and difficult process. Despite what most of us learned in school, this was true not only for those who were welcomed home from Vietnam with crippling indifference, but also for the "Greatest Generation" who fought the "Good War." It has also been true for those who have come home to warm handshakes and sometimes over-the-top displays of gratitude and acclaim since the terrorist attacks of September 11, 2001.

Don't believe me?

William C. Menninger was the chief psychiatric consultant to the Surgeon General of the Army from 1943 to 1946. Soon after the end of the Second World War, he observed that "most veterans were not 'problems' in themselves, [but] it would be playing ostrich not to recognize that they had problems, both big and little ones." One of the bigger problems for many was dealing with the fact that they had given some of the best years of their life to the military, sometimes without receiving much in return. A veteran of the war in the Pacific, for example, told a reporter shortly after he returned home that he realized he had "lost three years out of [his] life, playing catch up in school, catch up economically, catch up." His old friends, he discovered, had graduated from college. Two were doctors. All had careers they were proud of. "I was so bitter," he continued. "You wouldn't recognize me." When he separated from the military, this young man was advised that his wartime experience as an infantry sergeant qualified him to be a "Maine hunting guide." Instead, he became "a drunk and a wild man." He had no direction, no ambition. "I was just overwhelmed with bitterness," he said, "and full of hate and envy." This sense of disillusionment was so widespread among the sixteen million men and women who served in the American armed forces during the Second World War that according to a survey conducted in 1947, almost half of them felt that their military service had been an overall negative experience.

In 1946, a writer for *The Journal of Higher Education* warned that although many of the men who were now enrolled in colleges across the country had come home from the war more mature, with "a sober, realistic idealism, tempered by experience… eager to work for the ultimate goals they cherish," others were bristling with resentment. That attitude, according to the author, brought about "general restlessness and dissatisfaction which extends to their class work, their instructors, and their fellow students." Many of the veterans, the author continued, "resent the civilian attitude toward the war, with its complacency, its indifference to what is going on in combat areas, and its selfish considerations. Some men are inflamed over the relatively high salaries and the comparatively luxurious standards of living which men in civilian life have had in contrast to theirs in the Army."

Then there was the war in Vietnam.

Many of those who fought in Vietnam came home and were reviled as unwelcome relics from an unpopular war.

Dr. Jonathan Shay is a clinical psychiatrist who has worked with thousands of Vietnam veterans since the war ended and has written extensively about its lasting effects. Here's how he described the shameful homecoming many veterans were subjected to:

> They returned home to protesters who accused them of being torturers, perpetrators of atrocities, and baby killers. For every returning veteran who encountered this personally, there were many more who saw scenes selected for their dramatic and/or outrageous qualities in the TV news or heard nth-hand stories. The media presented a barrage of images portraying the Vietnam veteran as crazy, drug-addicted, and violent. For many veterans who had joined up because they thought it was their duty as citizens, who had grown up on John Wayne and Audie Murphy, rejection by the community was infuriating.

Philip Caputo was a Marine platoon leader in Vietnam attached to one of the first combat units to land in Da Nang in 1965. Not unlike those who came home from previous wars, one of the biggest challenges he faced was dealing with the fact that those at home didn't seem to realize, or even care, that America was at war:

> I used to get reactions of inexplicable anger, almost a fury, that would just come over me like that. When I was first going out with this girl who's now my wife, we were in a restaurant one night. I was shortly out of the Marines. I remember we were in a restaurant and I was looking at everybody, and I knew what was going on over there. I still had all sorts of buddies of mine who were over there, and in fact I had recently heard about one who had gotten killed. And I was watching everybody eating dinner and they were all well dressed and everything, and she said, 'What's the

matter?' And I said, 'Let's get out of here. In about two minutes I'm going to get up and start busting heads.' And I said, 'I don't know why.' I wanted to go there and wipe that restaurant out. It was so strong in me. My whole body was tensing up.

"And that was followed in about an hour or two by this black depression," Caputo continues, "almost like I felt guilty about feeling so infuriated that I got very, very depressed about the whole thing. And I was undergoing those kind of side waves, emotions going like this, all the time, to the point where there was a period in my life where it seemed like the only emotion I was capable of was rage."

"I'd go to a public place where people my age, it was business as usual or it appeared to me to be business as usual," says Dean K. Phillips, who was awarded the Silver Star and two Bronze Stars as a paratrooper with the 101st Airborne Division in Vietnam. "And I thought to myself, *Jesus Christ, you know, one of my best friends is blown in half and I keep thinking about that and here is this fucker sitting over here and the most important thing in his life appears to me to be whether the Dodgers win the pennant.*"

Fast forward to today. According to a 2011 Pew Research Center study, about half of all Americans admit that they have not been even marginally affected by the wars in Iraq and Afghanistan. Think about it: Since 9/11, the American public has been largely insulated from the realities of war in the Middle East. Indeed, with tax cuts, no sense of collective national sacrifice on behalf of the war effort, and with less than 1 percent of the American population taking up arms to fight, we've become a nation "at peace with being at war," in the words of David Carr. It's this lack of shared sacrifice that can be particularly difficult for today's veterans to deal with. In fact, according to author and documentary filmmaker Sebastian Junger, the most destructive challenge veterans of the wars in Iraq and Afghanistan face "is the sense that their country doesn't quite realize that it—and not just the soldiers—went to war."

Because so few of us have served—or even know anyone who has served—since 9/11, we have to look to the media to inform us about veterans and military service. The problem, of course, is that the media often traffics in tragedy and has a tendency to paint veterans with one of three broad brushes. "One story," writes veteran David Eisler, "is about healthy, hard-working, disciplined, well-trained and experienced veterans who would be an asset to any business or organization. The other tells of broken, disabled, traumatized veterans who have physical and behavioral health issues and require constant care and supervision." The third story, I would add, portrays veterans as dangerous, "ticking time bombs." In the wake of the Fort Hood shooting in April 2014, which left three dead and sixteen wounded at the hands of a "battle-scarred" soldier, for example, some media outlets, unwittingly or not, portrayed veterans as potentially violent and maladjusted. Some accounts even claimed—without citation—that the effects of post-traumatic stress "can range from temporary readjustment problems to suicide and murder, both of which have reached alarming levels among soldiers returning from duty."

To be fair, these three narratives do have some basis in reality. Some veterans are indeed heroes in the truest sense of the word. These men and women have been awarded the Congressional Medal of Honor and other awards for bravery and conspicuous gallantry, or have survived battles of overwhelming odds. Other veterans have returned home debilitated sufferers of traumatic brain injuries and post-traumatic stress. Depending on which studies you read, anywhere from 11 to 30 percent of veterans who served overseas claim to experience post-traumatic stress.

That may sound like a lot, but it's hardly a majority—certainly not enough to justify the impulse so many civilians have to inquire about veterans' mental health. At the same time, some veterans have fallen through the cracks and ended up addicted to alcohol or drugs, jobless, or living on the street. Sadly, it is also true that some come home and commit violent acts of aggression or choose suicide over life.

The comparably humdrum tales of veterans returning home, going to school, getting a job, and trying to make something of themselves simply aren't tragic or inspiring enough to garner much front-page attention.

The problem with many of the stories that do make the papers, however, is that they emphasize three equally useless messages that for many serve as representative of all veterans: (1) that veterans belong on a pedestal, (2) that they are troubled and need our sympathy, or (3) that they need to be feared. For those with no direct connection to the military, the competing sensationalist narratives we are spoon-fed present a seemingly unsolvable paradox that unfortunately widens the gap between the military and the civilian world. The truth, of course, is more complicated than that.

For those who haven't ever served, the gap between the military and civilians can be easily ignored. For those who have served, the military-civilian divide is everywhere and affects how veterans are able to relate to their families, their classmates and coworkers, and their communities. In contrast to past generations of veterans, many of whom were civilians drafted into service, all 2.6 million who served in Iraq and Afghanistan chose their path. While more than half of World War II veterans felt bitter because their wartime service set them back from their civilian peers, our current generation of veterans has internalized their distinction from the rest of society. They are the 1 percent, and they see that difference as a mark of honor. According to one recent poll conducted by *The Washington Post,* of the more than 2.6 million men and women who deployed to Iraq and/or Afghanistan, 90 percent said they would still have joined, even after considering all they now know about war and military service.

At the same time, however, my students realize that being alienated from the people they protected will only make their transition more difficult than it needs to be. That's why, we believe, the onus is on veterans to tell their stories—to help bridge the divide. For this edited collection, I asked my students to write about themselves and what they have experienced. I asked them to help you, the reader, better understand what it's actually like to be in the military, to go to war, and to come home. With thoughtfulness, humor, and honesty, some students have chosen to relive for you some of the worst memories of their lives and expose their trauma to the light of day. Others have taken a more academic approach, using research and other veterans' perspectives to help illustrate common issues veterans of all generations have had to confront. Still others have decided to tell you stories of what it means to serve, things they think you should know. As you will see, some feel they had important roles to play in the Global War on Terror. Others feel they mattered little. Some miss the simplicity and fulfillment of combat, while others never saw combat or saw enough to know they don't ever want to go back. All have made themselves vulnerable in the hopes that you'll respond with empathy and respect.

Despite their initial reluctance, my students have taken the initiative to help bridge the gap that divides them from those they fought to protect. In telling their varied and important stories, they reveal the common humanity we all share. Above all else, they realize that if they never tell their stories, we as a society will continue to see them as incomplete stereotypes—heroes or victims or monsters. What they want instead is for us to see them for who they really are—truly diverse individuals who made great personal sacrifices in good faith.

THE FIRES THAT MOLD MEN INTO WEAPONS

By Chase Vuchetich

"I want you guys to understand." He stared at the wall as the lights on our headlamps flickered. "You might have to kill women and children…. Can you do *that*?" His fire was out; even with the light on his face, his eyes were black as if there was no soul left inside. He was twenty-one years old. His clothes were filthy and tattered. Although he couldn't grow much more than a ratty mustache, he looked like an old man, tired and beaten down. We sat in a room that would soon be home for some of us, and would soon be left behind by others. Those who had called this place home for the past several months were finally going home, and they were trying to give us any advice they could think of to keep us alive. The only lighting was from the headlamps we wore. I stared into his still black eyes. Seconds passed, though it felt like hours, as we searched for the words to respond. Now we understood the place we were in. We would not be killing uniformed soldiers or even some simple "towel heads," as your common redneck fuck-head might say. We would be trying to kill an ideal in the bloodiest place of a country pumped full of drug money harvested from its own ground. Those we were replacing left the next day, but I wondered that night if they would really ever leave. Would I?

We come from small towns hidden in the hills, in the snow, or in the red haze of the desert. We come from large cities that spread like a disease across the country. Every place has a different story with the same plot. Everyone wants to leave these towns, but most of the time the military is the only way out.

I was a Navy brat, but only for the first couple of years of my life. I was born in Oak Harbor, Washington in 1991. At age three we moved to my Dad's hometown, Park Falls, Wisconsin. I would start and finish school there. I noticed something about that town as my class got smaller and my friends moved away. Every time someone got the opportunity to leave, they took it and almost never came back. Several of my friends decided to join the military.

I played football and wrestled through most of school. I learned discipline, respect for authority, teamwork, leadership, and what it meant to stick up for brothers. I was a normal kid, except for one thing: I had a fire burning inside me. My retired Navy parents had laid the wood in the pit. On September 11, 2001, I was ten years old, sitting in my homeroom class when another teacher came bursting in saying something about the World Trade Centers. We watched it on the news in our small classroom. Someone had just poured gasoline on my pile of wood.

At the beginning of my junior year, I was having some difficulty deciding what I wanted to do with my life; I still am. At first, I thought that I wanted to be an Apache gunship pilot in the Army. We went to a nearby high school for what they called a "college day." There were booths set up from schools all over the state. I was in luck, though—the recruiters were there, too. I immediately went to the Army recruiter. He stood there in his Army Combat Uniform (ACUs) with pens on his sleeves. I didn't understand at that moment how trashy that looked. I spent ten minutes watching him hit on girls while ignoring me before I finally got pissed and walked away. As I walked down the aisle of tables that were set up, I noticed the Marine Corps recruiter.

He stood there straight and proud in his dress blues. No one was talking to him. It was like there was a bubble around him, preventing all but a select few from seeing him. Being from a Navy family, I was hesitant to talk to him, but I approached him anyway. It took maybe two minutes, and I had the utmost respect for this man. His tone was stern but welcoming. He wasn't pushy; there was no sales pitch. He was just there to answer my questions, and after a while we just shot the shit. I was hooked.

He had just lit the match. I went home and broke the news to my parents that their son was going to be a Marine. They were shocked and made me promise to talk to all the recruiters. I did but never took them seriously. The Air Force guy who showed up to my house was fat and wearing khakis and a polo shirt. I saw him and thought, *Seriously!?* Although his command presence was weak and he lacked professionalism, he piqued my interest when he started talking about Pararescue. He did not, however, understand them or what they did. I knew after talking to him that I was going to be a Marine, though I didn't know what job I wanted to do.

I thought my Marine recruiter was a pretty kick-ass guy, so I thought maybe I would serve in K9 Military Police like him. Then I thought I might be a diesel mechanic. Both of these jobs would set me up for careers after the Marine Corps. But then I looked at my strengths and what I liked to do. I was an athlete, always have been. I needed to do something physical. I couldn't possibly fly a desk. The monotony would kill me. I was also an excellent shot. My first memory is sitting next to my dad at his reloading bench, where he would make ammunition and listen to George Thorogood and the Destroyers' "Bad to the Bone." By age five I had my own single shot, bolt action, .22 caliber rifle with peep sights. I was lethal with that rifle; no soda cans survived the day. Looking back, it's as if my childhood was that of a warrior class all along.

It became very clear to me one day that I needed to be an infantryman. Why wouldn't I be? I wanted to be successful, and that was the best way to do it. I told my parents a couple days before my recruiter came over with the paperwork. It was not easy for them to accept, but they knew I was doing what I really wanted, and they couldn't change that.

After passing my physical, I was officially enlisted in the United States Marine Corps. Less than a year later, I shipped out to San Diego for recruit training. Although being heavily intoxicated and having not slept at all the night before, I was ready to go! Boot camp was a breeze for me. My high school football and wrestling coaches were hard-asses, so the physical aspect of training was a cake-walk. It was harder to be away from family and friends for the first time more than anything. I graduated as a private first class the day before Halloween and was recognized for being the company high shooter in rifle qualification. After coming home on leave and realizing my ex-girlfriend had cheated on me, I was ready for the School of Infantry (SOI).

I arrived and immediately thought I was in hell. Boot camp was easy by comparison. If you did what you were told, no one screwed with you. SOI was all about getting you out of that mindset. Now we were learning how to properly and safely employ weapon systems and to shoot, move, and communicate with each other. It was winter in California while I was there, so all the rain and cold just made me miserable. I made some lifelong friends at SOI, some of whom I'd be with in my new unit.

"What's your rifle qual score and PFT?" The platoon sergeants and squad leaders were having themselves a draft. If you could shoot and run fast, they could use you. We stood with our backs to a wall and waited to be picked. I was picked second by a monster of a Marine based off my stunning good looks; that's what he said at least. I was to be in 1st Platoon Bravo Company, 1st Battalion, 5th Marine Regiment. I was put into a barracks room with another kid from Wisconsin. After dragging our sea bags to the barracks, I found my room on the third floor. There were drunk Marines standing in their doors trying to razz us as we walked past. We were told to get inside and not to open our door for anyone until morning. This was not a problem; our door didn't open. We had to crawl through the window.

The next day I was informed of the history I just became a part of. I was in one of the most decorated units in the Marine Corps, second only to 3/5 Darkhorse, our brother battalion. I was heavily encouraged to research my unit in past battles. By that I mean, if I didn't learn it, I would feel the pain from my seniors. I felt incredibly proud to be a part of something so much bigger than myself. And finally, after being in the Marine Corps for almost six months, I was going to get to learn what it was like to be an infantryman. Most of the things I learned in SOI, I was told to forget. It was time for "big boy" rules. Marines can't be machines anymore. We need to be thinkers because in today's battles *every* step you take, *every* person you meet, and *every* car that passes could kill you.

I had a year to prepare for our upcoming deployment to Afghanistan. There were rumors every week as to where we would go. All we knew was we were going. The closer we got to deployment, the more new guys showed up and combat vets would leave. We started to notice we had almost no combat experience in our lower ranks. Learning how to fight like a combat vet without ever having been there would be our only option. We also had to learn to trust each other so that when we had to, we could operate without hesitation. This crucial mindset would ultimately save several lives. We also became the closest-knit platoon anyone in that platoon had ever been a part of. We knew our jobs. We could locate, close with, and destroy the enemy in our sleep. It became not only our mission, but also our fuel. In a few short months, the government would pay us to go to a shithole country with no cell phones, no Internet, and no free time. They turned us into instruments of God's judgment. We were going to kill people for a living.

We left our small part of Camp Pendleton in the middle of the night. It's tradition in the Marine Corps for Marines to shave their heads before their first deployment. Only seven of the more than forty Marines with our attachments had been in a firefight in either Afghanistan or Iraq, so there were lots of shaved heads. But with a platoon commander who had been in the Recon community for fifteen years, a platoon sergeant who had been in Fallujah and was possibly one of the smartest people I know, and three very qualified squad leaders, we knew we had nothing to worry about. We were the best platoon in our company. Hell, our squad was sponsored by the owner of CamelBak! We thought we were untouchable.

After arriving in Camp Leatherneck in Helmand Province, I was shocked at how vast that base and its other half, Camp Bastion, were. There were men from all over the world there to fight with us. British, French, Australians, even Gurkhas from Nepal. It became very clear that the United States had some friends in this fight. We received a Rules of Engagement briefing from a JAG officer. I wanted to walk up and sock this asshole in the face. He made it a point to tell us if we slipped up, we'd be spending the rest of our lives in Leavenworth Prison. As time passed, we grew tired of Leatherneck and all the Marines unlike us. They were POGs (persons other than grunts). All we wanted to do was go to our area of operations (AO), Sangin. We had watched videos of the British and 3/5, the unit we were to replace, in Sangin. The British took their heaviest losses of the war there. We knew we were about to spend the next six months in Hell on Earth.

As we were approaching our company's forward operating base (FOB Inkerman, or "Ink"), the helicopter was using its onboard countermeasures as a precaution. We got off the bird and ran into the base with all our gear. I will never forget looking over the wall and seeing the dozens of white Taliban flags flying throughout the surrounding villages. I went from thinking *"holy shit, I'm in Sangin"* to a more realistic combat mindset. I was there to do what I signed up for—to fight and kill the people who supported killing innocent Americans. That night we would push out to our patrol base (PB Fires), and I would get to see one of my best friends, Josh Cawthorn, who had gone a month early with the advanced party.

Cawthorn had gotten in a firefight the day before while he was on patrol with the platoon we relieved. He said they fought like cowboys, fearless and with ferocity. He also proceeded to call us "boots" and told us about gunfighter names. His was Brother Horse Rising Sun. I never did find out where that came from. Due to the IEDs saturating the battlefields, our patrols and tactics were severely limited. The first man in every patrol had a metal detector and the second man—the 2 man—would mark the safe path. In certain areas men walked in footprints of those in the front in case the lead man had missed one. Cawthorn said at one point, the two machine gunners were stepping over Marines who were lying in the prone position, firing their M240s and screaming, *"Die Fuckers!"* This platoon had gotten in a firefight almost every day for the last six months, even after they had taken so many losses in the first two weeks of being at Fires that they were declared combat ineffective. They should have been relieved, but instead, they refused to be extinguished by the crafty and relentless enemy. In every engagement, they would unleash hell.

They would go as far as to make themselves vulnerable to draw enemy fire, and soon... so would we.

We would go on only a couple of patrols with the platoon we replaced. They showed us where all the fighting would go down. At one point in an area known as "The Hot Gates," where we were almost guaranteed to get into a mix with the enemy—where iron sharpens iron—one of the team leaders kicked back, lit a cigarette, and opened a can of orange soda. I thought he was out of his mind. There we sat, exposed and in a horrible position to return fire, praying they would ambush us... but nothing happened. They even tried to find an IED for us so we knew what to look for and what not to look for.

They also gave us the "bad juju" rules of Sangin. Bad juju rule number one: Never look for IEDs. You'll find them the wrong way. They would know. Their battalion had been hit time and time again by these explosives made from fertilizer and other materials. Number two: Don't trust anyone that isn't in your platoon, even interpreters. As if the locals weren't bad enough, sometimes the interpreters weren't there to help us. Number three: It's better to be judged by twelve than carried by six. This means it's better to pull the trigger on a possible threat and face charges for war crimes than for you or a brother to be killed instead. Mind you, I was only twenty years old while being faced with these decisions, and some were younger. Above all other bad juju rules, there was the famous advice of General James "Mad Dog" Mattis: "Be polite, be professional, but have a plan to kill everyone you meet." We were in a place where, every day, women and children were responsible for planting IEDs, spotting patrols, and gathering intelligence on us. We were fresh from the States, where people have a false sense of security, and they would take advantage of that.

Instead of fighting us while we had the experienced guys there to help us, the enemy waited until 3/5 left. They knew it when the hardened veterans were leaving. They knew us replacements probably didn't know what to expect. It was an opportune time anyway. Historically, every year the Taliban stops fighting once winter comes so that they can save up money and men to get through the poppy harvest. Once they sell all the poppy gum to the drug lords in the spring, they can finance their war again.

We were bored. There was no fighting. The only action we had was dealing with the kids who ran around asking us for "choclit" (chocolate), dollars, pens, and cigarettes. We played pranks in the PB. One night we caught a kangaroo mouse and Cawthorn put it in a mortarman's sleeping bag. I told my friends to stop asking for fights.

On May 12, 2011, my squad prepped for an average midday patrol following a very intense sandstorm a few days prior. We headed out the west gate, and I was the last guy. As I entered the first tree line, still within sight of the base, I bent over to pick up the bottlecap marker that we used to mark a safe trail, and I noticed a battery with two wires between my feet. How had everyone walked over this without it going off? I looked up at the Marine in front of me and said, "Hey Nevo… chow is right the *fuck* now!" At first he didn't believe me, but I told him to tell our team leader to get the engineer. I remember thinking there was no point in freaking out. If I was going to die, I may as well do it with a smile. My idiot team leader came back frantic: "Vich, are you okay? Don't move!" I shook my head and responded, "I'm fuckin' fine, just go get the sweeper." The engineer came back and at first accused me of wandering off his trail. After I showed him the bottlecap, he realized he led the entire patrol over this IED.

Before the explosive ordnance disposal (EOD) guys got there, the engineer told me to back up slowly and step on a little tuft of grass while he got some more guys to set up security. The engineer then went back up front and hit an IED that was just barely offset. Lucky for him, he walked away with a concussion and some road rash on his legs. Shortly after that, EOD showed up and found that the pressure device for the IED I found was under the tuft of grass I had stepped on. I guess it wasn't my time.

There was a village across the Helmand River from us that we called Tatooine (yes, like in *Star Wars*). We decided that since the village never got patrolled, most likely the Taliban lived there. So on the anniversary of the D-Day invasion, June 6th, we helo inserted into this shitty village and searched every square inch. Little did we know that the bastards were some seriously crafty individuals and managed to get all their contraband items out of town or hid them as we approached. One of my best friends, LCPL Nic O'Brien, and I were in an overwatch position in a cemetery. We sat on that hilltop all day in the beating sun, talking to pass the time. We also played with my range finder, guessing how far away different things were. For a couple of hours, our squad corpsman joined us and played "Never Have I Ever," where you are forced to admit things about yourself or things you've done no matter how embarrassing, trusting that it will never leave the ones playing. We talked about our families. By the end of that day, Nic and I knew every possible thing there was to know about each other. We planned our lives out that day.

On the evening of June 9 we left for a night patrol with the rest of our squad. Nic had been our lead sweeper since the engineer was hit. We went out the same west gate through the same field. This time, we headed past a mosque that was hidden by trees. Just as I walked out of sight of PB Fires, Nic was walking over a pipe used as a footbridge by locals. The pipe was metal, so his metal detector was useless at detecting the bomb buried next to it. We were complacent. Other than the one IED strike we sustained weeks before and some firefights to the east of where we were patrolling, we thought we were unstoppable. We all took another step forward. That's when I heard the explosion and saw the cloud of dust. When everything settled, there was nothing. No body. Nothing. We searched for him for maybe ten or fifteen minutes. It seemed like days. Cawthorn was also hit. He lost his eye. When I came up to help Doc Chavez, Cawthorn's face was already bandaged, but Doc wanted me to put pressure on and talk to Cawthorn to keep him awake. I asked him questions about his family that I knew the answers to and talked to him about his dad, who was also a Marine. He kept asking about Nic.

Doc Chavez will forever be one of my brothers. He had love for us that none of us will understand. As I was talking to Cawthorn, I heard a team leader screaming at the Taliban that he was going to kill them all. Moments later, I heard that they found Nic's body submerged in a canal. I was relieved for him in a way, because it would've been worse to be captured and tortured. One of my best friends had been sent to Valhalla—a place the Vikings believed only the bravest of warriors who die in battle go.

Nic was a hero, and three more were CASEVAC'd. Even after getting the reputation as the best squad in the battalion by our leadership, we had just been cut in half, including the following billets: our lead sweeper, the 2 Man, a machine gun squad leader, and our own squad leader. Three days later, on June 12, our platoon would hit four more IEDs, again just past sight of our posts. After another Killed in Action (KIA) and several more Wounded in Action (WIA), we were starting to understand how 3/5 had been beaten up. Three days later, on June 15, again my platoon hit two more IEDs. In a week's time, our patrol base of fifty Marines had sustained two KIA and twenty-one WIA. Several of the wounded were missing limbs or digits, and Cawthorn had lost his right eye. I will forever be in their debt. Every single one of them physically left a part of themselves there. Yet somehow I came back with only a bee sting for a battle scar.

Our platoon was relieved for three days and sent to Ink to get our wits and properly prepare for the two memorial services. I was one of the speakers for Nic. I was terrified that I wouldn't do him justice in the allotted time. After all, he loved to bust my balls for my horrible public speaking, so why wouldn't it be me doing the speech? At this point, every unexpected sound made us jump: a controlled detonation in the distance, a buckle on someone's pack, or even someone opening a can of soda. It was draining to be so terrified that you or your buddy's life or limb would be taken. To this day, I get anxiety while anticipating an expected noise, and my heart skips for the unexpected. I don't expect it to ever go away. While we were at Ink, a squad from Charlie Company took over Fires and also had a mass casualty IED strike.

After our three-day break and having a new company commander, we released the beast born from the burning infernos of our souls. We thought we flew into Hell when we got there, but really we brought it with us. We became blood-thirsty and every day was a manhunt. Two of our squads went to a patrol base just north of us and got in some of the fiercest firefights of our deployment. My squad went back to PB Fires. We had another squad there to help stand post so we could patrol. One day we took two four-man teams of EOD techs and the battalion gunner, Chief Warrant Officer Marine (yes that's his real name), on patrol with us.

A couple days prior to this patrol, EOD had found over twenty IEDs in the surrounding tree lines of PB Fires. To disrupt the enemy, we set up along a canal we called the Mississippi because it separated the fighting from the only peaceful village in our area of operations. We detained a random guy on a motorcycle (according to our new standard operating procedure, anyone on a motorcycle was considered hostile) and EOD had found a couple IEDs, including a twenty-pounder (twice as big as the one that killed O'Brien). As they began to search an adjacent tree line, we came under the largest ambush my squad would experience. We were in a textbook U-shaped ambush that included at least one belt-fed machine gun and one bolt-action sniper rifle. LCPL Harper and I were with the detainee in the Mississippi, and twenty yards away were Sergeant Hodge, our squad leader, and PFC Carly, our current machine gunner. Twenty yards from them was the rest of the squad. The four of us were pinned down by cross fire from the U-shape. As the snaps of the soviet rounds broke the sound barrier over our heads, we heard Sergeant Hodge yelling to us. I poked my head up over the side of the canal and saw him pinned down in the same cross fire, and the bolt gun was nearly hitting him.

I noticed that there was a nearby mound of dirt, so I told Harper we had to go get the detainee to that mound. I looked at this simple Afghan and pointed up and said, "Get the fuck out." He shook his head and sank into the water. Harper jumped up on the side of the berm and grabbed him as I pushed him out by his backside. They began to run over to the berm and I thought to myself, *This shit is crazy!* I took a deep breath and pulled myself out of the canal, and blacked out. I don't remember running to the berm, probably because I was scared out of my mind. I only remember waiting to feel the 7.62 round they fired rip through my body. I took a knee behind the berm and immediately started looking for shooting positions. Then I remembered that I was in Sangin, and that the Taliban knew we would look for such things and place IEDs there. I decided to stay on my knee and risk getting shot. My hunk-of-shit M249 machine gun jammed several times and continued to keep me out of the fight, but with Harper's suppression and spotting, Carly was able to lay down the hammer on the marksman.

Gunner Marine was next to a couple of close friends of mine: LCPL Greig, LCPL Reyes, and LCPL Carey. Reyes, or "Jon Jon," was pinned down so badly that every time he tried to move, a burst of machine gun fire would tear apart the ground in front and to the sides of him. Greig was laying down some very surgical fire to places that the Gunner wanted. Carey told us later that at one point the Gunner told him, "Carey, take over the fight, I'm going to condition one dip." In the middle of the worst enemy fire I had ever encountered, he was taking a moment to put a dip of tobacco in. I swear, if you look up the term "badassery," Gunner Marine's picture would be there.

During the debrief of that patrol, the Gunner told us that after being in a firefight with every squad in the battalion, and on several combat deployments (seriously, I think he had been on about seven deployments already), he had never seen a squad in a mix with that amount of enemy shooters in that well-organized of an ambush conduct themselves so calmly and effectively. We were back. We felt great, and we wished the rest of the squad could've been there with us. Still, we began to change, though we would not realize it for a few more months.

On September 15 I was standing post when Corporal Michael Dutcher came up with a plate of food. He gave it to me and said, "Here, take a break." I thought he was kidding. Dutcher was my first team leader when I got to the platoon. He was always the type of noncommissioned officer we could approach with any problem. I told him he was a sweetheart, took my Kevlar helmet off, sat down, and enjoyed a breakfast for a change. He gave me ten minutes of peace to myself in that shithole where I didn't have to think about someone trying to kill me. After I came off post, I got my gear ready for patrol and got a few hours of sleep. Dutcher went from post straight to patrol.

The sweeper in his squad was sick, so he volunteered to do it for the day. My platoon commander gathered my squad and told us Dutcher had been killed by an IED. I felt completely numb. I asked myself, "Why wouldn't it be Dutcher? Why wouldn't he be dead? After all, it is Sangin." At that moment, I knew I would never be the same. While Dutcher was following a local down what should've been a clear path, the local jumped over a canal and started running. Corporal Dutcher took his last steps trusting a man he thought was there to help him. Exactly one month later, we returned home.

The day my company returned to the United States, we had a homecoming on our regiment's parade deck. There were hundreds of people there to welcome us back. Families, girlfriends, brother Marines from other units, even a Patriot Guard escort to the base from the airport. While walking up to the parade deck in a mass formation, I could see my family and friends standing behind the rope. My dad wore his dress blues for the first time in almost twenty years. My mom had lost a considerable amount of weight and looked great. The second I saw them, though, I was overcome with survivor's guilt, and I wasn't comfortable being seen as or treated like a hero. I felt numb to them. The only people I wanted to see that day were my friends who had been wounded and could not return to combat. I didn't want a parade of bikers, or a big party on the parade deck. On my mind were my friends who could never again take the footsteps to their families, some of them there or still in hospitals, and some never to return. Why was I given a second chance at life over them? As I walked closer, there was a force pulling me back. I wanted to go back, go back to the place where I was supposed to die. This is something I have struggled with.

I didn't realize it yet, but I was on a path to alcoholism and several other problems. At this moment, however, I am happy to say that my drinking is under control, and I'm making sense of what I've been through. Though I will never completely understand the things that happened in Sangin, I can cope with my memories for now. We also never broke the Geneva Conventions, and for that I am grateful. Above all else, I served with some of the most amazing people on the planet, and for that I am thankful. As for the fallen, we continue to honor them every day. Till Valhalla, warriors.

AUTHOR'S NOTE: *I wrote this for my brothers in 1st Platoon and so that those who have never had to endure combat can better understand what we go through and who we are.*

MY NEW RITUALS

By Josh Thunder

Step 1: Measure out sixty-five grams of green coffee beans. Step 2: Pour the green coffee beans into an air popcorn popper and put the lid back on. Step 3: Turn on the air popper and start the timer. Step 4: Monitor the beans and take note of the first audible crack that is heard. During the roasting process, you will hear two sets of audible cracking noises. They are called first crack and second crack, respectively. Anything after the first crack is drinkable. The closer you get to the second crack, the darker your roast will be. Step 5: When you've roasted the coffee to your preferred darkness, shut off the roaster and pour out the beans into a metal colander. Step 6: Immediately shake the colander in front of a fan, in order to cool the beans, halting the roasting process. Doing so also removes any chaff that could have been around the beans. Step 7: Package the freshly roasted coffee in glass canning jars. Do not tighten down the lids all the way, because during the first twenty-four to forty-eight hours, the coffee will be off-gassing CO_2. Step 8: Within two weeks, use your favorite brewing method to enjoy newly roasted coffee.

Since leaving the Army, I have found that the things I love doing the most are things that I would not have enjoyed doing before I joined the military. I have packed my free time with tasks that some might see solely as repetitive. There is something more to these tasks than simple repetition. For me, I enjoy the concentration that is required. I find it fulfilling and satisfying. In the midst of a "repetitive project," I am able to turn my mind off to the worries of the world around me and focus on the task at hand. When I can concentrate on even a single aspect of a project, striving to do my best, I am at peace. Time has stopped, and I have forgotten all my worries.

I read an article in *Alive: Canada's Natural Health & Wellness Magazine*. The author, Brooke Broadbent, said that "mindfulness helps us realize that we can create our own happiness—or unhappiness. We understand that we can feel peaceful deep inside, although chaos seems to rule supreme around us." I believe that when I engage in everyday tasks, I am participating in mindfulness by focusing on the task itself. Broadbent summed it up when she said, "Mindfulness can be practiced in a variety of ways. Basically it refers to being intentionally aware of your thoughts and actions in the present moment, without judgment."

During the day, I find that my mind wanders easily. Instead of focusing on my classes or the work I have to do, I often think about specific things that I'd rather be doing. I've started roasting my own coffee, primarily to save money, but also because I like to have fresh beans around instead of the stale Folgers they sell on the grocery shelves. My mind continually wanders to the different aspects of the roasting process. How can I better utilize the beans that I have? Could I get a home roaster and monetize my hobby? Could I do it for a living?

I'm not sure if my mind has actually been changed or if I'm just predisposed to enjoying repetitive, concentration-intensive tasks, but I do feel different now that I'm out. I need the tasks to give me a sense of accomplishment, a sense of pride in the work I'm doing. The order that we submit ourselves to while we're in the military is almost completely lost once we get out. While I was in the military, we had to get up at a specific time, and we didn't have say in it. We had tasks that we didn't have say in. We had to be at different places, sometimes for extended times, and we didn't have a say in it. Once we disconnect our lives from such a rigid structure, there is an overwhelming sense of freedom that we aren't used to having. I can't speak for everyone, but I needed something to simulate that need for structure.

I recently read a *Navy Times* article that said, "Many troops and veterans are finding relief from PTSD symptoms in recreational hobbies such as model-building, horseback riding, yoga, shooting and even knitting." I don't have PTSD, but I still think that my life has been altered, and I think I am in need of relief from daily life. In the same article, the author talked about a group of veterans who went on a therapeutic fly-fishing trip. Rasul Mowatt, an associate professor at Indiana University has said, "There's something compelling—something we saw in veterans from multiple wars—and all responded favorably to the experience, even commenting how they preferred this experience to other forms of treatment." He went on to say, "Early research indicates that maybe we should consider treating with traditional programs, but maybe offer alternatives that veterans can sign up for, whether it's basketball leagues, fishing or riding. Each have yielded some successful response from veterans." I think order and a sense of brotherhood, as well as the mindfulness involved, are important to veterans once they are on the civilian side of life.

To take a glance at the ways soldiers coped with transition in the past, author Marcus Brotherton interviewed T.I. Miller, a ninety-two-year-old World War II vet, about his experiences when he came home from the war. When Brotherton asked, "What helped?" Miller said, "My wife and family were a big help, especially my wife, Recie. At the same time, it's something you gotta just do yourself. The secret, I found out, is just to stay busy. There were no government programs to help back then. No therapists to see. Nothing like that. I was born and raised out in the country. So after I came back from the war, I built me and Recie a house out there close to where I'd grown up. I got out there and roamed around in the mountains. That's what helped."

"One time," Miller continued, "they closed the mines down for three months. Someone said, 'Where you gonna go look for a job?' I said, 'I ain't. I'm gonna spend the summer out in the sunshine.' And I did. I took a two-pound double-bladed axe and walked a half mile up above where I lived. We had a field there, and I cut down big trees and cut them into fence posts. All I had was that axe. I made my own mallet and split those trees myself. I got me a half acre of ground, plowed it up, and had a field. That same summer I grew potatoes, corn, and beans. The whole summer I spent growing things I wanted to. I'd be out in the woods at daylight. I just worked like that and built myself back up."

Brotherton pointed out three "key actions" that Miller took. First, Brotherton explains, "He busied himself with straightforward, non-emotional work." On numerous occasions, that was exactly what I needed. For this past Thanksgiving, I wanted to help my mother fix dinner, and she said I could help by peeling potatoes. She was fixing dinner for twenty-two people, so the pile of potatoes she needed peeled was no small pile. Still, I enjoyed peeling from the first to the last potato. Second, Brotherton continues, "He got active, outside." Since the semester began in September, I've been riding my bike to and from classes. I find the exercise and fresh air to be incredibly helpful in burning the stress of the day away. Third, Brotherton finishes, "He could see what he accomplished each day." Whether it's peeling potatoes or roasting my own coffee beans, there is a tangible marker of what I have accomplished in a set amount of time. I like that. It makes me feel proud of what I've done. Put these three practices together, and I think they serve as a great model that all transitioning veterans should consider as they try to cope with their new situations.

More examples of veterans turning to concentration-rich environments come from a *Des Moines Register* article I found recently that was written by Christopher Doering. In the article, Doering talks about veterans who are leaving the military and entering the agriculture and farming business. In the article, Christopher interviewed Mike Simester, an Iraq War veteran who left the Army and went back to Iowa to farm. Simester said that farming is his "forced therapy," because "every morning, regardless of how bad I feel physically, or how tired I am, there is still stuff that has to get done. The animals have to be taken care of, the irrigation has to be run." Simester started Serendipity Farms four years ago in Muscatine, Iowa even though he and his wife had no prior agricultural experience. As for me, I grew up on a small beef farm in Wisconsin, and as much as I hated it growing up, I am drawn to it whenever I have free time. The simple-sounding life of a farmer is anything but. There is a vast amount that one must know in order to be a successful farmer.

I've been spending some time at my parents' farm, helping out with chores. I'm not sure I would want a full-fledged beef or dairy farm, but I wouldn't mind dabbling in some form of agriculture. I like the traditional idea of the family farm with one cow for milk. My wife and I have talked about gardening, raising our own chickens, and maybe a few goats. Nothing fancy, but enough to subsidize our food bill. The idea of working to produce our own food would meet an overwhelming urge I have to be somewhat self-sufficient. Being able to know what I'm putting into the food my family is eating is enough reason for me to have a garden and a few animals.

For his article on transitioning veterans, Doering also interviewed Chris Brown, an Iraq and Afghanistan War veteran who left the military and now teaches other veterans how to farm organically outside of Seattle. The produce that Brown's farm grows is then sold at the city's VA hospital on Thursdays. According to the article, "The time on the farm with other veterans, he said, has helped him cope with his post-traumatic stress disorder and reduce his anxiety. Brown's fine motor skills, which were affected after a mild traumatic brain injury suffered in Iraq following a suicide bombing, have improved following hours spent harvesting, planting, and pruning. He now sleeps better at night." More specifically, Brown told Doering, "That type of reflection can be very powerful for me after so many negative things, so much death and destruction. Just in that aspect, [farming] is therapeutic." I think a large portion of the activities that I engage in, while shutting off my brain and allowing me to focus, also allow me to do my own reflecting. I think this time is important to my transition because I can really evaluate what is important in my life.

One of the first tasks I engrossed myself with after leaving the military was building a wooden display box for my brother's 1911 handgun. My brother was getting married a little over a month after I got out, and I wanted to make something really special for him. I had never done any woodworking as substantial as this, but I knew that this was what I envisioned giving my brother. During the countless hours I poured into the project, I had plenty of time to think. I realized a long time ago that being close to my family is very important to me, and while I was producing this gift, that thought was only reinforced.

***

Every morning in the military, I would set my alarm to wake up with just the right amount of time to not be late for physical training. I knew down to the minute what time I had to leave in order to get to work. I was all about making the most of the little free time I had. I would skip going to breakfast just to get half an hour more sleep. Maybe that was my ritual then because I think I already had enough structure in my life from the military. Whatever it was, I didn't feel the need to structure my life any more stringently than the Army already was. Now, I love a great breakfast every morning. I make sure to wake up early in order to make the best meal possible. There is something about my new morning ritual that I find comforting.

I start by putting the bacon on the stove before I start the coffee. By the time my coffee is finished, it is the perfect time to put on a few eggs. Scrambled or fried are my go-to methods of cooking them, although I am finding more all the time. I'm not sure how anyone could skip breakfast. Not only does it give you the energy to be productive during the day, but it is also so much better than waking up, throwing on some clothes, and running out the door.

I don't have any solid argument as to why I do the things I do. I feel different, but at the same time, I've always felt this way. Mindfulness is a recurring theme in my life now. Even though I was only in the military for four years, it felt like an eternity. It felt as if that was all I had ever known. Now that I'm on the outside, I don't even do things the same way I used to six months ago, in the midst of the end of my stint in the military. I always thought I would stay the same forever, that my interests wouldn't change, but I have found that thought to be false. I have a new sense of being now that I am out. But that's just fine with me. I'm enjoying my new rituals.

YOU'RE... WELCOME?

By Leon Valliere

"Thank you for your service." It's the superficial, knee-jerk response when a civilian hears that you've served in the military. All service members and veterans have at some point gone through this same awkward conversation with complete strangers. For the most part, the conversation ends there, unless you're really lucky, like I was. My most embarrassing instance of this happened when I was visiting home for the first time after leaving for the service.

I had been stationed in Pensacola for my advanced training, and I was heading home for the Fourth of July celebrations. I had only been in the Navy since the past December, so I had hardly any real experience. I wanted to travel home in uniform because this was the first time my family would see me in it. I was wearing my Navy Service Uniform, which looks similar to the Marine Corps Class B. It is comprised of a khaki top, black slacks, and a garrison cap. The uniform also has a ribbon rack, where I flaunted my two ribbons. I had the Navy Marksman Ribbon and National Defense Ribbon, which showed that I had no real experience yet.

I arrived at the airport with a little over an hour to spare. I walked sharply to the ticketing booth and got my tickets printed out. The airport was packed with people with an air of desperation. Everybody looked on edge and anxious to get to their flights.

I made a little small talk with some flight attendants as I walked toward the security checkpoint. The checkpoint was overflowing with people hurrying up to wait. The line for the metal detector zigzagged across the terminal space. I wasn't in much of a rush because I arrived early, so I posted up at the end of the line. I like to think that my military training helped me block out the white noise of monotony. I quickly got that blurry haze to drown out my surroundings and waited in line.

That's when I got tapped on the shoulder.

A TSA officer had been trying to get my attention and walked across the threshold of passengers to talk with me. He mentioned a TSA Precheck lane that I should move into because I was in uniform. This line essentially skipped all the crisscrossed nonsense that all the civilians were in. This was the first time I had encountered a military perk outside of paying less on my cellphone bill. I grabbed my carry-on bag and sauntered past the clearly upset horde.

I loaded my bag on to the x-ray scanner, took off my belt, and emptied my pockets. I knew even before the metal detector that I would be stopped. I was wearing my two ribbons proudly, and the ribbon rack is metal. I also had shirt-stays on, which have metal clips that connect to the bottoms of a uniform top. I was anticipating being stopped, and I honestly wasn't too worried about it.

With my boarding pass in hand, I stepped through the metal detector... ding.

The same TSA officer who helped me before asked me to step aside. "Sir, are you carrying any weapons?" *No, I wasn't.*

"I need to wand you just for security purposes." *Yeah, that's fine.*

I was then asked to step into this taped off box on the floor and to raise my arms above my waist. This was all expected, so I complied and stepped aside for the civilians to pass through the metal detector. As I raised my hands, I began to scan the crowd, and I made eye contact with an old salty looking man. He was wearing a hat with an American Flag on it, and he didn't look too happy. He frantically shouted, "Don't you dare search him! He's a god-damn American war hero!"

I honestly wasn't expecting anything like that to happen and neither was the TSA officer. After that one voice of dissent, the crowd started to chime in about how the TSA should be ashamed of themselves. I was still standing with my arms raised as the TSA officer used the magnetic wand. Ding.... The wand chimed on my chest. I explained the metal in the ribbon rack fixture. Ding.... The wand chimed over my legs. "Sir, do you have shrapnel or metal in your legs?" the TSA officer asked. The closest I had ever been to getting fragged was in *Call of Duty*. I explained the metal in the shirt-stays. The whole search lasted maybe thirty seconds, but that old man was glaring daggers into the TSA officer.

After I was cleared, the TSA officer directed me to my gate and said, "Thank you for your service." He pronounced every syllable and said it loudly enough for the older man to hear. I think he was saying it just for the sake of the pissed-off civilians. I put on my shoes and belt and grabbed my bag. I had to get the hell out of there before some hysterical civilian offered me a Bronze Star.

I had a solid forty-five minutes before my flight at this point. I figured I should bleed out the most time to avoid another rogue wave of patriotism. I waited until the final boarding call before I made my way to the jet bridge. My ears were still slightly scarlet, but I had a while to calm down from the security checkpoint. After scanning my ticket I started to walk down the jet bridge with a sense of relief. Again, that haze started to settle in as I boarded the plane. I recognized one of the flight attendants I talked with earlier. She was doing the preflight checks and smiled at me as she headed to the cockpit.

I didn't think much of it as I started to make my way to the final row in the plane.

I was lucky enough to get one of the last seats on this flight, but it was all the way in the back. The other passengers were busy fumbling to store their carry-on bags. I was in the clear—there was no chance for another embarrassing moment. That's when the intercom cut through my zombie-like state.

The captain was speaking to the passengers: "We at Delta would just like to thank our onboard military members for their service to our country. With a special thank you for the Marine boarding the plane now. Thank you, son." I had just passed the first class cabinet when the announcement stopped. Now I had the privilege of walking the gauntlet of economy class with all these civilians thanking me for my service. I wasn't even thanked for being in the Navy, which was especially unsettling.

That was the longest walk I've ever taken, with all the half-hearted "thanks for your service" phrases and pats on the back. I just wanted to get to my seat and sleep at this point. All the way to the back of the plane... right next to the bathrooms and flight attendant galley. The cute flight attendant finished her preflight checks and took her special seat next to me. I scored some free drinks and a phone number on one of the most patriotic travel days of the year. The perks of being a god-damn American war hero, I suppose.

SEE ME FOR WHO I AM

By *Geoffry Norfleet*

I am a walking Discovery Channel with a military background, and that is how I want people to see me. I want civilians to see me as knowledge—an outlet to the world. I want them to look past me physically and emotionally. I want them to crave what I have in experience. There are some who may argue that at twenty-one years old, I am still a child. At least that's what some senior said to me recently as I was walking out of my intro to psychology class. It took every ounce of my being not to make him eat the dirt underneath the snow. Even if age were a factor, I know more now than he ever will. It might be a little egotistical and slightly narcissistic, but I felt like I was better than him in that moment. I felt like I was better than him because he jumped to the assumption that I was a true freshman because I was walking out of a freshman-level class. He was ignorant and acted on his ignorance, thus upsetting me.

Instead of seeing me as a tattooed veteran or some freshman child, I want people to see me for who I am—a walking Discovery Channel with lots of stories and experiences to share. Above all else, serving in the Army gave me perception. I got to see the world and have lots of amazing adventures. In fact, I have more stories to tell about each of the countries in Europe I visited than I do about my deployment to Afghanistan. When I was stationed in Germany I got to have some great times with my brothers snowboarding down the mountains in France and Austria, bar hopping in Poland and the Czech Republic, and enjoying the finer things in life at the museums in France and Spain—and everything in between.

I have so much knowledge to spread, but when most civilians find out I served overseas, the only thing they want to know about me is whether I ever killed anyone. Do you know what it feels like to get asked a question like that? It's a shame how blind people are and how content they are being as such. I want people to ask me where my favorite place to visit was, or what my most memorable moment as a soldier was. I want them to ask me about the food and the cultures I have seen. I want them to ask me about the people and the nightlife. I want them to ask me anything and everything, except "Did you kill anybody?" To me, it is a narrow-minded and ignorant thing to ask.

Before I begin to define myself on my own terms, I want to tell you a little about myself. Maybe once you better know me, you'll understand that there is a method to my madness. I was born in a very small town called Sulphur Springs in Texas, which is about an hour outside of Dallas. My mother had me when she was very young, and she worked a lot so she could keep food on the table. We lived in a small house very close to her parents, who also had a hand in raising me. I can't remember a single time that my parents had to tell me to get outside. I remember leaving in the morning and not coming back until the sun went down. Even when school started, I would get off the bus and play outside until I heard my mom yelling for me. This is why I'm thinking I chose to be infantry; I couldn't see myself cooped up in an office behind a desk.

I had a pretty average childhood: friends, the neighborhood, the toys, the works. Then my mother met a guy and they started dating. At first I thought he was a pretty cool guy, but maybe I was blinded by all the presents he was buying me. At this point I was cut off from my father and didn't end up seeing him again until I was eighteen years old. When my mom and her new boyfriend got more committed, I got uprooted from all my friends and the place I grew up so that we could move to Bettendorf, Iowa.

I count this as the second chapter in my life, a new story in my book of life. At first I didn't like Iowa because I was from Texas and had an accent. I was picked on very harshly. This is where I started to become a more independent individual who didn't take crap from anybody. I started getting in trouble a lot, because I would get in fights with anybody who said anything less than the best of me. After much discussion among counselors, my parents, and me, we decided to find an outlet for me to focus myself and teach me some discipline. This was the beginning of my new life.

I found wrestling, and I quickly fell in love. I loved the contact, the structure, and the sense of brotherhood you feel when you're part of something larger than yourself. I learned very quickly and started going to most of the meets. I even made my first friend in Iowa. He was also a wrestler and a couple of years older. He even convinced me to join the Boy Scouts, and we grew very close. Everything seemed to be looking up for me; I was making friends and staying out of trouble. I was also winning meets—well, some of them, anyway. There were some very good kids who had been wrestling since they could walk. Anyway, everything seemed to be turning around. Then my parents had another child, my little brother Ben. A couple of years later they had another. Then another change came in seventh grade. I was again uprooted and moved. It was really hard for me. Facebook didn't exist at the time, and Myspace wasn't big, so I lost all connection. Not having a friend is very hard on a child; not having connections with others makes you feel very alone. Or at least it did for me.

The next chapter of my life starts in a small village in Wisconsin called Rosholt. I was once again the outsider and didn't make friends easily. I eventually made a friend named Nikki who was from Oklahoma. I could relate to her, so we got along. Wrestling season came up that year and I joined, made a couple more friends, and seemed to start fitting in. I then found a friend, Orin, who is now like a brother to me. I started spending a lot of time at his house with his family, and this was when I met one of the most influential people in my life. His dad, ex-military, now a cop, had all the answers and just seemed like he had it all figured out. Just in time, too, because that is the point in everyone's lives when the teachers start asking you what you want to be when you grow up. Looking back now, I just laugh, because I thought I had it figured out. But I'm now attending school, and I realize I still don't really know what I want to be when I grow up.

We grew really close, and his family became mine. The closer I got to my friend's family, however, the farther apart I grew from my own family. It just seemed like I didn't belong there, and my step-dad was always treating me differently. When I turned 18 I got into a really bad fight with him, and I packed my bags and left. Orin and his family were more than happy to take me in. It was senior year, so I took care of myself, helped around the house, and tried to figure out the rest of my life. It was then that I decided to join the Army. Orin picked the Air Force. Most of our friends were going into the service as well. We had a buddy go into the Navy and two others joined the Air Force. I didn't tell my parents about my decision. They didn't even know when I left for basic training.

This new chapter in my life landed me first in Fort Benning, Georgia, where every infantryman does his basic training. I thought I was going in very knowledgeable because Orin's dad had filled me in on some of their tricks and the things they do to "mind fuck" you, as they would call it, trying to weed out the weak quitters. I had wrestled pretty much all my life and played football here and there, so I was physically and mentally prepared for the life change. They first put us in a place called 30th AG, where we just sat around and learned new things, stood around and learned new things, and didn't sleep and learned new things. They were trying to get us ready for actual basic training and make sure we weren't completely new to the information they would be teaching us there.

After being there for about a week and a couple of people dropping out, we were sent to Sand Hill, which may as well be where Hercules himself was trained to be a warrior. To this day, it molds the best of the best who serve our country. They call it Sand Hill because it is literally that, a giant sixty-five- to seventy-degree-grade hill made of sand that goes on for about 800 meters. The drill sergeants called it the widow-maker. We all got used to it, though; you could only run it so many times in a day before you just didn't care anymore. They trained, molded, and shaped us into infantrymen for the big Army. After graduation, I found out that I would be shipped off to Rose Barracks in Germany—the next step in my life. I was a little upset at first, because I had finally found a family I fit into, and I wasn't going to see any of my friends again for a really long time.

I received ten days of leave to go back and see family before I was to report to my new duty station. I felt like a whole new person when I got back. I was very proud of what I had accomplished and thought everybody else would be too, but most of my friends had already left town. The only people left there were the people with no purpose or drive, and those just weren't my kind of people.

The military experiences I had in Germany were pretty run-of-the-mill. We went to the field a lot, which sucked because there are only two seasons in Germany. There is the winter season and then the thawing season, and that is no joke. I started out as a gunner on an M240 Bravo. There is nothing like being eighteen years old and having that kind of power. I was very good with this weapon system and shot top squadron a few months later, receiving my first Army Achievement Medal. After being there for a while, I was switched to being an assistant gunner. The assistant gunner carries the ammo, tripod, and extra barrel. Being an assistant gunner sucks. Carrying that much weight killed my feet, but it forced me to get big quick. I graduated high school at just shy of 150 pounds, but while I was in Germany I ballooned up to 200 pounds real quick. Most of this weight was in my legs. I couldn't find pants to wear anymore, especially in European brands.

After doing that for a little bit, I was moved to vehicle commander, which means I was in charge of the vehicle platform that we were transported in. I was also in charge of the MK19 gunner system, which is a fully automatic grenade launcher. I did so well with this system that every time my platoon sergeant wanted somebody, he would pick me. I was in and out of positions until we finally got the chance to deploy to a combat zone. Being an infantryman in the Army and not deploying is like being a professional football player who rides the bench during the Super Bowl. I had to deploy. It's what I was trained to do. I told myself that if I didn't deploy, I was going to re-enlist until I did.

The next chapter in my life landed me in a place called Kandahar, Afghanistan. I remember the first day, landing in the C-17 on the runway on Kandahar Airfield. It didn't feel that hot to me because I could still remember what Texas felt like, but everybody else I was with was sweating and panting like dogs. It was just above one hundred degrees outside, and for anybody who has been there, they know the smell. At the end of the forward operating base (FOB), they have black water ponds full of sewage that wafts downwind over the entire base. I wish I could explain the smell, but there is really nothing I can think of that resembles it.

We downloaded our bags and sat around until they found bunks for us. Then we bunked down for the night and started training in the morning. I wasn't looking forward to that. In fact, the last thing I wanted to do was watch PowerPoints on the Rules of Engagement (ROE) in the middle of Afghanistan. The week went by very quickly, though, as did the rest of the deployment. It seemed like there were thirty-six hours in a day, but the weeks and months flew by.

The FOB that would be my home was known as FOB Lindsey. We entered it through a small gate with a tower that had a gunner in it. The base was surrounded by giant containers of sand and rubble known as Hesco walls and sand bag fortifications. It vaguely resembled what I imagine the great forts of the American frontier must have looked like. We were to sleep in tents that couldn't keep you cool when it was hot or warm when it was cold.

Life there was hard to get used to at first. There were many long, hot days with little sleep, but once we all got into a pattern, things started to fall in line. We didn't care about the lack of food anymore because we were getting care packages full of beef jerky, candy, and pretty much any snack you could think of. My life consisted of patrol, sleep, and making gains in a small gym that was on post when we got there.

When winter started creeping up, I was surprised. I had figured that it would be warm year round because of where we were located. I couldn't have been more wrong. The cold bite of winter came hard and fast. The days dropped from one hundred degrees to sixty or lower and the nights dropped from seventy to the thirties. It kept getting colder and colder to the point that we all looked like we were fighting a war in Canada.

At the end of every day, if I wasn't on patrol, I got to do my favorite thing in Afghanistan. My buddy Will and I would take a pack of smokes or a couple cigars out to the T barrier mortar shelter that was outside our tent, and we would play guitar, sing songs, and build a little fire. Sometimes others would hear us and they would come out and sing along or bring their guitars and play along. This was the best part of the day, every day, because for those two or three hours, we all forgot that we were in Afghanistan. We all forgot what we had done the day before, or what was coming up, and we were just living in that moment.

Still, there were moments that have stuck with me. One in particular took place during a mounted patrol through one of the villages that was on the outskirts of our perimeter. We were cruising down a very narrow road, and one side of the road gave way and our truck slid off into the ditch. Normally, the villagers would have started getting antsy, but these people were different than what we normally dealt with. The village elder and all the kids came out with shovels and ropes and other tools and waited for instructions. This was so different to us because in most of the villages we frequented, people would throw rocks at us or yell curses. It took us about eight hours before we finally got unstuck. The kids were a very big help. This was the point—about four months into the deployment—that I realized these people weren't all bad. They were just people trying to get by. We gave all the kids whatever we had on the trucks—candy from our MREs (meals ready to eat) and snacks and things of that sort. These are the good experiences I had and there are many like it. That is all I have to say about Afghanistan.

As for the rest of my time in the service, some of my fondest memories of being in the military involved weekend pub crawls, snowboarding trips, sightseeing, and sporting events. The reason I would much rather people ask me about where I have been is because I would rather take ten minutes and tell you my worst story of traveling than take an hour and talk about my best in Afghanistan. Education and exploration are so much more fun to talk about. For example, I always enjoy talking about my trip to the Alps in Austria.

Five of my buddies and I woke up early in the morning and headed out to Austria. When we finally arrived, we were so excited to go snowboarding that we just dropped our stuff off in the room, got dressed, and headed for the hills. Upon seeing the options for the slopes, we decided to take the second most difficult one because we were all soldiers, and there was no way anybody was going to catch us on the bunny hills. I already knew this was going to be hilarious because two of my buddies had never been snowboarding or skiing. It took us almost three hours to make it down the slope the first time. When we reached the bottom, two of them were done. They were tired from sliding down the mountain mostly on their faces or butts. The remaining three of us decided to go down again. About half way down the slope I wiped out pretty bad. I was just lying there thinking about life and how much my butt hurt when a child no older than four came flying down the hill. I will never forget this child. He was small and looked like he just learned how to walk, wearing a blue jump suit and shredding the snow. He got about two feet away from me lying on the ground, turned really fast, and kicked snow all in my face and down my shirt. I was so mad, but there was no way I was going to catch him. My buddy Yeazell came up and started laughing at me and making remarks I won't put on paper. I knew I could catch him because I was way better on a board, so I got up and started chasing him. He made it about 200 meters before he scorpioned, landing on his head and taking out two skiers in the area. He laid there for a minute and said his head really hurt and that he was done. Later we found out he got a concussion and was pretty messed up, but it was funny at the time. The final two of us decided we would go down one more time, and we flew. We made it down the mountain in sixteen minutes. The night was followed by bar hopping and a long drive in the morning.

Prague, Czech Republic is the most fun place I have been—and probably ever will be—in my entire life. Prague is one of the party capitals of the world, so you can only imagine the craziness that goes on there. In all the time I spent in Europe, I went back to Prague five or six times. None of those times left me with anything less than a story I won't be able to tell my children until they are grown. During my first visit there, four of us went on a pub crawl called the Drunken Monkey, and we ended up playing beer pong against a bunch of Brits and Irish gentleman, who we wiped the floor with. Every time I went, I met new people and fell more in love with the city. The weekend before I left Germany, I went there one last time. I had the time of my life. The owner of the pub crawl, who was in love with us as much as we were with the city, got us VIP treatment everywhere we went, and at the end of the night he closed the bar, and we had a massive party. It was truly a night to remember.

If people ask me where the best place to go and see cool things is, I will tell them Barcelona, Spain every time. Besides being a very beautiful city next to the ocean and having a wonderful culture with wonderful food, the architecture there is insane. My personal favorite is La Sagrada Familia, also known as Gaudi's cathedral, which is on the outskirts of Barcelona. It was made to resemble a forest, and it was truly nothing like anything I had seen before. The outside looked like poured concrete that was roughed to look like a tree canopy with many ornate statues and towers. On the inside, there were many more pillars than any other church or cathedral or even castle I had been to. All the stained glass work was in shades of the forest and the colors bounced off the pillars and really made the biggest cavity of the cathedral feel like a forest. Right outside that was a garden that was designed by the same person who designed the cathedral. It was so abstract and unique; I would love to visit again someday.

Birds of a feather flock together, and a flock of geese is worse than one, especially if it is pissed. The same can be said for soldiers. When I'm alone, I walk and talk and act in a professional manner. I try to smile and be polite. But as soon as I get united with a flock of my brothers in arms, especially 11-series Infantry guys, I am a whole different person. Every stereotype has an ounce of truth to it, and the stereotype that infantrymen are rowdy, strong-spirited, hard-headed fighters has some truth to it. It's not like I change for the worse, but I force myself to change for the better when I am not with these guys.

In his widely influential book, *Man's Search for Meaning,* Holocaust survivor and psychiatrist Viktor Frankl writes that "when we are no longer able to change a situation, we are then challenged to change ourselves." My civilian life is like putting on a mask of humanity for the general public so that they don't see how this goose really acts when he is out of the cage. Now, I'm not saying that we get crazy or turn into serial killers or any of the other bullshit that the media spews all over the place. I want our veterans and our military to be known as the most professional force in the world. It is really sad to say that I know we are not and never will be, but I want civilians to think we are. And it is even sadder that I have to wear a mask and act like somebody else to prove that we aren't who the media says we are. I have seen soldiers come together and accomplish amazing things, but it doesn't matter. The positive things we do get drowned out by the stories of the veteran who got too drunk—apparently we all have drinking problems—and beat up a guy who talked shit to the wrong person. It's like trying to get first place and we started in the losing bracket. The soldier at Fort Hood who went crazy and killed half a dozen people was in the news for months, but did you hear anything about the various vet groups around Texas that teach hunter safety and gun safety without pay so that the state doesn't have to fund it? Nope, not a damn thing.

The most recent chapter in my book of life landed me in Stevens Point, Wisconsin. I am attending college there and have changed my major three times already. I thought I was going to grow up to be a psychologist, but then I realized I don't have the patience or the tolerance to listen to average Joe's normal day-to-day problems. I changed my major to personal health and wellness promotion because I love the gym and the fit life. After much thought, I then changed my major to occupational therapy. I decided I might as well go all the way and not half-ass my career choice.

I have days of mind-numbing boredom where I do miss the military life; however, I enjoy where I am in life and have no regrets. My connection base is building and I truly feel like I have nearly integrated back into civilian life. The veteran community really helped as well. I had a strong connection with these guys because they were just like me and I didn't have to wear a mask around them. I didn't have to watch my tongue, and we could talk about the things we went through and share stories. I found a niche that I fit in and rode with it.

In his book, Frankl concludes, "Those who have a WHY to live can bear with almost any HOW." In my conclusion, my "why" is this: I have knowledge of the world—or at least the places I have been—and I would love nothing more than to share it with everybody. All they need to do is be open-minded and ask.

ATTITUDE IS EVERYTHING

By Sean Casey

At my going away party, my master guns (master gunnery sergeant) said, "I want to read about you someday," and he meant it. Master Guns Carter could see my drive, persistence, and commitment to excellence, because he's the one who developed and instilled those skills in me. When I arrived at Marine Corps Forces Europe in Stuttgart, Germany, I was an idiot—as all "boots" are—with very few skills and even less wisdom. I made bad decisions, drank uncontrollably, and spent money like it was on fire. I did all this because I was a young man without a mentor. Even worse, I had little direction or purpose attached to my life. I had said multiple times during this lost period of my life that I would be happy if I even made it to thirty because I wanted to live hard and fast. I didn't spend much time in the Marines acting like this, because leaders like Master Guns Carter, motivators like SgtMaj (Sergeant Major) Green, and some sharp knife hands from SSgt (Staff Sergeant) Sanchez made damn sure I became the best possible version of myself.

My days of living reckless came to a sudden halt one night in Germany. It started as most nights did for me: waiting around for some of the Marines to wake up or get bored enough to go downtown and have a few drinks. Marines don't get a lot of time off, so during our much-needed days of rest, we usually slept as much as possible to charge up for the next week. As soon as we had a crew of people to go out, everyone would start getting ready. I'm a guy, so I was ready no more than five minutes later. The Jersey Shore wannabes who called themselves guys usually took a bit longer than me—like two hours longer. I didn't usually hang out with these particular Marines, but I really felt the need to go out that weekend—even if I didn't like the crowd.

It was at that point that I started pre-gaming like any savvy Wisconsinite would do if someone else started cutting into their free time. I got too drunk too quickly, because German beers are usually twice to three times as large as American beers and have roughly twice the alcohol content. This is a bad combination for a young man who believes he is invincible.

I ended up going out that night and I remember walking into a club. That's it. I can't remember a single other thing that took place that night, and that lack of memory was incredibly disconcerting to me as I sat in a jail cell. The German police (Polizei) had picked me up while I was sleeping on a park bench. The Polizei usually left people alone as long as they didn't cause a ruckus of some sort, but since it was February, and I was rocking a t-shirt, they felt it was necessary to prevent hypothermia. I appreciated their concern until I saw Master Guns enter the building. Master Guns truly embodied the Marine expression "No better friend, no worse enemy." He's the first person I would pick to fight along my side and the last person I would want to fight against.

Master Guns stared at me with pure hate and discontent that made me feel as if I was about ten inches tall and made out of paper-thin glass. It was absolutely humiliating to know nothing about what had happened and worse yet, what was about to happen. He didn't speak a word to me for the first ten minutes of the drive back to base. Silence left me to my own thoughts, which raced around my head, circling the worst possible outcomes at the end of every decision I could have made. The silence grew to be anything but silent as my conscience's voice grew into a thunderously loud and seemingly uncontrollable disappointed parental figure. "Do you understand what this is going to do to?" Master Guns asked, finally detaching me from my own thoughts. I was so afraid that I could barely combine words into a sentence, so I defaulted to typical Marine responses. "Yes, Master Gunnery Sergeant." He made eye contact with me, making his point very clear without saying another word. I was up shit creek without a paddle, and the only way out was to follow every instruction he gave me with trust and confidence. That is, after all, what a good master gunnery sergeant is supposed to do—protect his Marines at all costs.

We arrived at the barracks, and he escorted me to my room. He then gave me the ass-chewing I expected. Imagine the feeling of hope like a porcelain doll. He hit my hope with a sledge hammer. He left abruptly shouting instructions as the door violently slammed behind him. I followed his instructions, just as he told me, with trust and confidence.

A day passed, and I was still in my room periodically getting "negatively counseled" concerning my behavior by every Marine who was senior to me at the time, which was everyone. Negative counseling is a Marine term that means getting yelled at for being a stupid boot. I didn't count how many Marines decided to diligently fulfill their duties that day, but man did they get a point across. I messed up, and I should feel bad.

While waiting for more knife hands to find me or for Master Guns to return as he had said he would, I heard a different kind of knock on my door. It was different because it wasn't really a knock. It was SgtMaj Green practically kicking my door down. SgtMaj had a thick southern accent accompanied by a worn out voice box from yelling for twenty-plus years at Marines like myself. He was always smiling too, which was very deceiving if he was disappointed in you. I rushed to the door, popped to attention, and everything else is unimportant. He yelled things, and I did things. After SgtMaj was finished acting like a crazed drill instructor, which he used to be, he told me to get in uniform and meet him on the parade deck. Rushing to get my uniform on as quickly as possible to ensure SgtMaj didn't wait any longer than he would like to, I looked out my window to see a formation—a formation that included every Marine, sailor, and civilian in our command. "OH, SHIT!" I thought. There is no other possible reaction.

I met SgtMaj outside the barracks. He was smiling because I'm assuming he could see my heartbeat through my clothes. He marched me out in front of the formation, crunching the frozen grass as we stepped it out. A formation usually looks like a group of concrete statues, never moving, perfectly spaced, with unwavering bearing. This formation, however, was shivering because they had been outside waiting for the guest of honor to arrive for about 30 minutes. SgtMaj called out a few Marines to be still and the rest attempt to follow suit. Then the motivated SgtMaj proceeded to embarrass me for what seemed to be a full decade, but was most likely just fifteen minutes. I did my best to make no movements, breathe evenly, and stare forward until my vision became a small tunnel of darkness, blocking out as much as possible. When he dismissed me from the formation, I clenched in frustration, pounded my heel to the ground, and marched off. I wish I could have kept walking to get away, but the Marines don't let you walk away.

"When the student is ready, a master will appear." I had been preached that sentiment by SSgt Sanchez for quite some time by the time I screwed everything up. "It applies now," he said. SSgt Sanchez was the most professional Marine I had ever met. He was by the book, persistent, and above all, motivated to succeed. When someone had a question, SSgt had the answer. Over the course of two days, I had been broken down to nothing—well, maybe a young depressed guy with some insanely large problems would be a better description, but I prefer the former. SSgt took me under his wing and became my mentor. Things began looking different after this.

SSgt and Master Guns set out to improve me and rebuild what they had broken. Master Guns oversaw the operation while SSgt executed every step. Looking back now, I'm not sure how I didn't notice what they were doing. I'm glad that I didn't. I was faced with one option: I was to succeed at every task they laid out before me, dedicate every hour in every day to the Corps, and above all, learn to lead.

SSgt kept my page 11 (disciplinary papers for kicking me out) pinned to the side of his desk as a reminder of the consequences for even the smallest mistake, and he threatened to send those papers out more than once. My motivators are fear, a challenge, or a subtle gesture of expectation, and they began to use them.

We tore up my page 11 six months later, and I never looked back. During those six months, I mastered my profession under the watchful eye of SSgt and broke a record for the fastest combat fitness test ever run at the command. Master Guns and SSgt brought me in for a meeting. The message was, "don't stop now." I didn't stop there, because I respected them too much. Unlike before, when failing one of their tasks would have gotten me kicked out of the Marine Corps, now I couldn't fail because I never wanted to see their disappointment like I did after that night. There's no going back to something so terrible.

SSgt Sanchez had reached his rotation date shortly after, and he was set to go back stateside to demobilize. This was my trial by fire—my testament of readiness. As a corporal, I was suddenly faced with the task of running not only my section of Inbounds, but also Customer Service and Quality Assurance. Our office was short by about six Marines. To put this in perspective, most corporals don't even run their own section, which consists of two to three Marines. I was by myself, alone, and unafraid thanks to my training. Two other Marines were in the office during this three-month struggle: Gunnery Sergeant Maxwell and Corporal Elwood were immensely helpful. Between the three of us, we were the administrators for every Marine in all of Europe and Africa. We succeeded with flying colors. Master Guns rewarded me with Marines. I was to lead them, which is undoubtedly the greatest responsibility anyone can have in the Marine Corps.

Young Marines are dumb. I can obviously attest to that, as evidenced by the decisions I made early in my career. That being said, I was recklessly dumb, but the Marines given to me were just dumb. One in particular—Green was his name—can only be described in this way: imagine Forrest Gump without the athletic ability. He was my gift from Master Guns. It took every last thread of my patience, but I made that sorry excuse of a human being into a respectable Marine after about a year. I have gray hair because of Lance Corporal Green, but I wouldn't trade it for the world. Being a leader is the toughest task in the world, and it is also the most rewarding.

I responded to Master Guns at my going away party, telling him, "You bet your ass you will, Master Guns," because that was his last task for me. The final thing he wanted from me was success on a different front. He didn't just build a Marine from that broken rubble, he built an attitude that will help me succeed at anything I put my mind to—an attitude thirsty for success and unwavering through hardships. An attitude that can do anything.

ONE DAY IN JULY

By Nathan Coward

My life's path has crossed with my father's past repeatedly and relentlessly, teaching me over and over again the difficult lessons of humility and the strength required to be meek. I realize now that the irony of my following in my father's footsteps had been lost on me for some time. Previously, I felt I was uniquely me, nothing like my father, but I see now that could not be further from the truth. In all reality, I am my father's son, and nothing could ever change that.

Growing up, I had no desire to follow in my father's footsteps. My dad had a difficult upbringing. The abandoned son of an Air Force father, with a drug addict for a mother, he spent the majority of his developmental years in a foster home. His foster parents were wonderful people, though I don't feel anyone could have reached him through all of the pain and anguish he felt as a child. Drugs, alcohol, anger, and aggression were the tools he chose to use to shelter himself from the pain of his past.

Though blessed with both my mother and father in my life as a child, the relationship between them was extremely rocky. Abuse, infidelity, poverty, addiction, and legal problems plagued their union, and it terminated in divorce around the time I turned ten. Their relationship remained on rocky ground even after the divorce, and it would have been a miracle if either spoke a positive word in the direction of the other.

In addition to the confusion the breakup of our family caused, being a child stuck in the middle of this intense hatred left me spinning. Confused, angry, and worst of all, hurt, I could not understand how two people I loved so much could say such awful things about each other. If each was as awful as the other said, was I wrong for loving them?

Anger and aggression. That's how I chose to respond to this confusion. My father had chosen the same path. To the best of my recollection, this had been the first strong instance of my present and my father's past converging. Growing up, I was quick to fight. I bullied other kids. I had to make sure that someone else felt as awful as I did. I reflect on that time in my life with considerable regret. I had no right to do to others what had been done to me. I had regrets then as well, which only intensified the confusion in my life.

It didn't take long to find a healthier outlet for all of this: football. That may be where my path first began to deviate from my father's past. It was a coping mechanism my father had not exploited in his youth. When I played football, I could let out all of my anger and aggression in an acceptable way. The aggression I had been using as shelter from the pain in my life was allowed to flow freely on the football field. Not only that, it was applauded! The more aggressive I was, the greater applause I received. By the game's end, the aggression I felt inside was exhausted in full. It seemed I had a natural affinity for the sport. For eight years I unleashed as much of this negative energy on the football field as possible. By the time I turned eighteen, however, it had become an outlet that just wasn't strong enough.

One day in July 2000, I received a phone call from an Army recruiter. Maybe that was what I was missing from my life, I thought. Maybe it would require an army, the U.S. Army, to teach me the discipline and structure I needed to be content.

I went in to meet with the recruiter, keeping it a secret from the rest of my family. I knew my mother would only cry and my father would expect that I join. I did not need this pressure or expectation to influence or cloud my decision. My father served for two and a half years as a cavalry scout in the U.S. Army in the late 1970s, and I wanted my decision to be mine, with no influence from my father or his past. I was attempting to construct my own unique path. Ironically, I was trying to do this in the same exact manner my father and his father before him had. Contemplating this time in my life now, I believe my mind had been made up even before I met with the recruiter. I was going to be a soldier.

The recruiter told stories of adventure and danger I could have never imagined. I cannot remember his name, but I remember he was an infantryman. I remember he wore a Ranger Tab on his shoulder. He was Airborne and Air Assault qualified, and his chest was filled with medals. He was also adorned with unit patches on both shoulders. At that point in my life, I couldn't envision anything more satisfying than being such a badass, a hero.

I told him I wanted to be the soldier out in front, the one leading the charge, an adroit and dedicated soldier. He advised me to follow the path he had traveled: join the infantry, complete Ranger School, Airborne School, and Air Assault School. He promised that this path would not only spawn an elite soldier, it would also teach me all of the discipline and structure I had been searching for.

I hurried off to the testing center to attempt the ASVAB— the military's aptitude test—and determine what job Uncle Sam would allow me to perform in his Army. When the results came in, I had scored in Category I, which qualified me for any and all of the military occupations the Army offered. That didn't matter, though. I chose the infantry.

My father dropped me off in Madison the day I left for the Army. During the car ride, he told me a little about his time in service and what I might expect. As I left his car I witnessed, for the first time in my life, my dad fighting to refrain from crying. His reaction created a feeling of stupefaction. He was a hard man, one who never admitted to feelings of love. And there he was, on the verge of crying. He admitted that he was proud of me. I told him I loved him, and I rushed off to the recruiter's office in fear of breaking down myself if I lingered much longer.

The recruiter drove all of the recruits, including myself, to Milwaukee to swear us in and issue orders. Soon I was off to Fort Benning for the rigorous training affectionately known as basic training. Four months later, I graduated from basic training, and along with that came my orders for my permanent duty station: Alpha Company (Commander-in-Chief's Guard), Fort McNair, Washington, D.C. Report date: 28 December 2000.

Fort McNair is the oldest active infantry base in the United States Army, and the regiment is the oldest active duty regiment. Alpha Company, steeped in tradition and history, was patterned after General George Washington's personal guard of that day. Fort McNair sits on one hundred acres and is currently home to National Defense University. Originally constructed in 1794, the base was overrun by the British in 1814 and rebuilt at the end of that war. Notably, Fort McNair was the site of the confinement, trial, and execution of Mary Surratt. Mary Surratt, who aided in the assassination of President Abraham Lincoln, would become the first woman to be sentenced to death in the United States. Stories of ghosts and hauntings on base were commonplace. In a house on base, where Mary Surratt was rumored to have been imprisoned, a handprint can be seen on an attic window outlined in condensation.

In the center of the parade field on foggy days, a large circular area, approximately fifteen feet in diameter, can be seen vacant of all fog. It was alleged that this is where, in a deep well, the woman and children took shelter along with the gun powder and fighting supplies for the base when the British overran Fort McNair. When the base was taken, a British soldier threw a match down the well, blowing everything and everyone in close proximity to smithereens. Stories of hauntings in the barracks among soldiers were also common, though I wonder if these stories were birthed largely as a result of excess alcohol consumption and hysteria.

Along with the duties of Alpha Company came the responsibilities common to the rest of the regiment: arrival ceremonies for high-level foreign dignitaries, burials in Arlington National Cemetery, wreath laying ceremonies at the Tomb of the Unknowns, presidential security details, and maintenance of the tactical proficiency of the infantry.

From September 11, 2001, through the end of November 2001, Alpha Company served as the primary search and recovery unit inside the Pentagon after the attacks. Though a gruesome and grueling detail to perform, I recall no complaints or instances of disgruntled behavior from any of my brothers, all of us doing our patriotic duty with pride and conviction.

After my time in service, my struggles to acclimate to "civilian life" did not differ much from my father's experiences. I did not delve into the drug culture like my father had, though I did spend plenty of time in the local tavern. The allure to feel accepted, to feel "normal" was the hold alcohol maintained over me. It wasn't until my father shared with me his struggles and strengths during a similar time in his life that I found the strength to let go of alcohol— that was my saving grace.

I had followed in my father's footsteps, and he had followed in his father's footsteps. Both my father and I had done this unwillingly and unintentionally—each of us writing a slightly different narrative, improving on the past in our own ways. The goal of any father is to provide greater opportunities for his children than he had been given as a child. Through sharing his experiences and allowing me to explore a path of my choosing, he had done just that. I will write my own future, but the song of my father will always sing its influence over how it will be written.

SERENDIPITY

By Ross Petersen

Serendipitous. That's how my story was described to me. After some thought, I would have to agree, because serendipitous basically means "coming into good fortune by accident." My story isn't completely based on chance, but major parts of it are. My story, as for most veterans, starts out in my later years of high school.

Sometime during my junior year, I received a letter in the mail from the local recruiting office. Like most juniors, I threw away the letters and didn't give them any thought. They were, however, quite persistent to say the least. Either that or I was too lazy to get myself taken off the mailing list. As I was unable to decide what I wanted to do with the rest of my life—which I think is too much pressure for an adolescent—I started to entertain the thought of joining the military for the education benefits. The education benefits had the most influence on me, because at sixteen or seventeen, I had never had a high sense of nationalism or national pride, not because I was un-American or anything, but because I had never given it any thought. I was pulled for two simple reasons: we were poor, and I was smart enough to go to college.

One day after school, I was taking the garbage out to our burn barrel. I was kind of stressed at the time because, as I said before, I didn't know what I wanted to do after I graduated. Burning the trash was stress-relief for me—something about watching the fire dance calmed my nerves. I dumped the trash, poured a liberal amount of lighter fluid on it, and set the garbage aflame. While I was being mystified by the elegant dance of the flame, I noticed a letter that said something like: CALL THIS NUMBER IF YOU WOULD LIKE TO SPEAK TO A RECRUITER type of letter. I was watching it burn for about a minute without any thought, and then, almost instinctively, in one motion I reached in, pulled the letter out, shook off the burning parts, went back inside, and gave him a call.

After some months of talking with the recruiter, I had to choose what my job in the Marines was going to be. Like most veterans, I contemplated joining the infantry, but my mom talked me out of it. She said she wouldn't sign the consent papers (because I wasn't 18 yet) unless I chose a non-combat MOS (military occupational specialty). I was at my cousin's house when my recruiter called and told me, "You need to choose a job now, or you're going in open-contract." Open-contract means the Marines choose your job for you. He gave me two options: intelligence specialist and field radio operator. I didn't really know anything about either of the jobs, so I let chance decide my outcome. Still on the phone, I picked up a quarter and spoke softly to myself, "If it's heads I go radio operator, if it's tails I go intelligence." It was tails. Intelligence it is.

More months passed. I graduated from high school. I went to boot camp a week after my eighteenth birthday, and I had some additional training after. In April 2010, I graduated from my MOS school. I then had to choose where my next duty station was going to be. We lined up outside the classroom, and one by one, we started to pick where we were going to spend the next two to four years. If I remember correctly, I had three options to choose from: 3rd MLG (Marine Logistics Group) in Okinawa, Japan; 2nd MAW (Marine Air Wing) in Cherry Point, North Carolina; and Marine Corps Tactics and Operations Group in Twentynine Palms, CA. I knew I didn't want Twentynine Palms, because I heard from senior Marines that bases in Afghanistan or Iraq were better than that place. That left me with two options: Okinawa or North Carolina. Not having a quarter handy, I did the next best thing my juvenile nineteen-year-old mind could think of: I used the eenie-meenie-miney-mo method. Basically, I used a child's counting rhyme to make a major life decision, which, unless you think about it and count the syllables of the whole rhyme, is an okay way of choosing things at random.

The next month, I got off the plane after an extremely dull fourteen-hour flight from Minneapolis to Okinawa. As the months went by, I got better at my job and leading new Marines; however, I still had not left the island (which is uncommon). I talked to my leadership, and they agreed to let me participate in the upcoming Cobra Gold exercise. Not long after, we went to Thailand to set up for the actual exercise, which started in the beginning of January and lasted until the middle of February 2011. Almost immediately after that, I was sent to participate in Operation Foal Eagle, which took place in South Korea from the end of February until the second week of March.

March 11, 2011. That was a date that will stick with me for the rest of my life. On that day, we received news of a 9.0 earthquake striking the coast of northern Japan, with the epicenter about seventy miles from the Oshika Peninsula. To add insult to injury, a tsunami followed immediately after. A couple of hours after feeling the aftershocks in Okinawa (almost 1,600 miles away), I was already briefing General Crenshaw on the situation. Within a day or two, we were mobilized to Oshima Island to help. Operation Tomodachi was underway.

Our job was to provide assistance in the form of clothing, water, food, shelter, and debris and casualty cleanup. The bond we—the Marines and the local population—had at that time was like nothing I've felt before, or since. The experience was surreal. Toward the beginning of May, the Japanese government stated that they would take care of things from there on out. So we said our goodbyes, wished them the best of luck, and went back to Okinawa.

Of all the things I've done in my service, this next part was probably my favorite, primarily because it has a happy ending and it was more personal. When I was in boot camp, the inside of my cheeks were swabbed for a DNA sample. That DNA sample was sent to a bone marrow registry—the C.W. Bill Young Department of Defense Marrow Donor Program. All of this was unknown to me at the time. In the beginning of September 2011, I received an email stating that I was a match for a thirty-three-year-old woman. I was asked whether I wanted to donate to a complete stranger. I said yes for two reasons: (1) I was able to get a week and a half away from the military, and (2) I was able to help a person and potentially save her life. A few emails and annoyed higher-ups later, I was on another excessively long flight to Washington, D.C. I arrived at the Lombardi Cancer Center at Georgetown University and began the six-day long process of donating bone marrow.

Before I say any more, I should explain that there are two ways of donating bone marrow. The one that is very invasive and takes marrow straight from the bones can be excruciatingly painful. Then there's the other way, which is less invasive. It's called PBSC (peripheral blood stem cell) donation. They give you a shot of a drug called Filgrastim in each of your triceps once a day for five days. The drug increases the stem-cell production in your bones until it leaks into your blood. On the sixth day, the doctors and nurses hook you up to a machine that filters the amount they need from your blood. The needs of the recipient determine how long you're in the procedure. The only pain I experienced was where the needles entered my skin, and minor joint pain from the increased blood volume. After the procedure was over, I went back to Okinawa at the end of September 2011 to finish out my time on the island.

In May 2012, I left Okinawa and I went to MCAS (Marine Corps Air Station) Miramar to finish out my contract. In April 2013, I received an email from a woman named Emily DeVillers. I had no idea who this person was or why she was contacting me... at first. As I read further along in the email, I found out she was the woman I donated to. We exchanged a few emails back and forth, getting to know each other. She told me of a cancer walk she was going to do in her hometown of Green Bay, Wisconsin, and she wanted to know if I could come.

I finished my time in the military and started to work in my local town of Luck, Wisconsin until September came along and I went to visit her. I showed up to the school where she teaches, and she immediately got teary-eyed, which was appropriate for the moment. She gave me a tour of the school. I met her sixth-grade class and her son Logan, who was in second grade at the time, and her daughter Addison, who was in fifth or sixth grade. After school, she took me out to some restaurant, and I had the pleasure of meeting her husband, Greg DeVillers, who could not have been happier.

At the walk I met some of her close friends and family. Her mother, Kathy Kauth, gave me a card and instructed me to not open it until I got home. After the walk, we said our goodbyes, cried a little, and went our separate ways. When I got home, I read the card, and it said, "Emily is... a mother, a daughter, a sister, a wife, a daughter-in-law... Emily is, because of you. Thank you so much."

I must've read it at least ten or fifteen times. The feeling I felt is hard to describe.

I bet my story probably isn't what you'd expect to hear from a veteran. No bombs or bullets, just a burning piece of paper, a coin-flip, and a child's rhyme. Serendipity.

A HISTORY OF TRANSITIONING

By John Elbert

It can be tough transitioning from the military to civilian life, especially after deployments. I have recently done this, but luckily for me, when I transitioned out of the military it was after my third deployment. I was used to transitioning to life in the United States after a deployment. It was my new normal. Many other veterans throughout American history, however, have returned home from wars and been met with difficult challenges and little help. One thing I've learned, though, is that many of them found ways to overcome their challenges, which has helped lead the way for this current generation of veterans.

The problems we see on the news today regarding the ways veterans are treated by society have roots at least as far back as the First World War. There are even similarities from that war to wars we're fighting today. In 1917, the British entered Baghdad as liberators and faced insurgents just as we did in the war we are currently fighting there. More than 200,000 U.S. soldiers returned home from World War I, many suffering from physical and mental injuries. By 1919, however, only 217 of those veterans had completed rehabilitation programs.

In 1917, the president signed into law the War Risk Insurance Act, which provided government-subsidized life insurance to veterans. The former president, Theodore Roosevelt, wrote a letter to the drafting committee of this amendment, saying, "It marks a great step forward. It puts the United States where it ought to be, as standing in the forefront among the nations in doing justice to our defenders." The act included a dependent's pension in the case of death or injury as well as a $60 (about $850 in today's dollars) discharge allowance at war's end in recognition of service rendered. Wisconsin enacted the Wisconsin Educational Bonus Law of 1919, which provided $30 ($420 in today's dollars) per month to veterans so that they could attend any nonprofit educational institution. The federal government attempted to follow suit by entitling all veterans to one year's vocational training.

During the Second World War, about 16 million Americans served their country. Before he died in 1945, President Franklin D. Roosevelt said that those serving "must not be demobilized into an environment of inflation and unemployment, to a place on the breadline or on a corner selling apples." To help prevent such a possibility, the president proposed a payment and a year of college or other training, as well as unemployment benefits to all veterans upon leaving service.

Not all programs to help veterans that came out of World War II were really helpful, though. During World War II, 1.2 million active-duty troops were admitted to military hospitals for combat fatigue (what we call post-traumatic stress today), almost double the number who were hospitalized for battle injuries (about 680,000). In 1943, VA Assistant Administrator George Ijams pushed urgently to get approval for a procedure known as the lobotomy, thinking it would help cure those suffering from extreme forms of combat fatigue. After World War II, over 2,000 veterans were lobotomized, meaning that they had their prefrontal cortexes separated from the rest of their brains. A doctor named David Merell later said, "Looking back at it, it was a terrible thing that came out of the psychiatric medical field." Mistreatments like these have led to many veterans having a great deal of mistrust toward federal programs aimed at helping veterans.

In many ways, the veterans of the Second World War faced the same challenges many returning veterans today face. Betty Nichepor, a female World War II veteran, once said that

> I was married to Al, in a new city, with a new family, and new adjustments, just like everyone else after they came out of the service. A lot of adjustments. Changes in your lifestyle. It's hard to come from military life to civilian life for everyone I think. Interesting, to learn, in the military your food was free, and your housing you pay very little for it. Then you come back and you have to get your own clothes because you have military clothes, you buy your own food and you have to learn how to cook. Which I don't like to do [ha-ha]. It's a big jump from what you were doing to what you did when you came back. Adjusting to married life was one thing and learning how to become a civilian. It's easy in one way but it's hard in another way. I don't know how to explain it. Leaving... I was happy to leave but ten years later I wished I was back in the service. It wasn't so bad that I hated it but it sometimes you think—oh gee [in the military] everyone was doing things for you and you were just doing your duty, but when you're a civilian you're doing everything for yourself. It's a change... you have to do your own laundry, big change.

Leaving home, going to war, and then coming back is like starting a completely new life with completely new and different challenges, and then shortly thereafter going back to your old life, which is now a completely different life where everything is new once again. Though the times have changed, the struggles facing returning veterans remain very similar.

After the Second World War was over, many returning veterans came home to one of the greatest welcomes in our nation's history. Towns threw parades welcoming home their troops, and people genuinely thanked them for what they had done. Economically, World War II soldiers' lives were made much easier in material terms than in prior wars. Their transition from soldier to civilian was supported by an unprecedented number of government programs, ranging from educational benefits to low-interest loans and medical care. They were also allowed up to fifty-two weeks of unemployment at $20 a week (about $260 in today's money.)

After World War II, the nation seemed to begin to lose its love for those who serve their country. As soldiers returned home from the Korean War, much less attention and gratitude was given. The Veterans' Readjustment Assistance Act of 1952 restricted eligibility requirements for veteran benefits and programs and reduced the amount veterans could receive in benefits. For example, unemployment compensation was cut in half, and educational benefits were reduced. There was also very little public attention focused on that war. Once they returned home, most veterans were not applauded. Some were even scrutinized for having communist sympathies. Most were more or less simply ignored. It was not just civilians who ignored those who fought in the Korean War. Veterans from previous wars could be just as harsh. Some veteran organizations even denied memberships to Korean War veterans because their war didn't "count." One veteran said years later, "I guess it was an unpopular war. It wasn't considered a war, just a police action. But to the fellows who were there, it was a war, and we're here not for us but for the guys we left in Korea." After hearing stories from my grandfather of what it was like fighting the Chinese in Korea, I would say that the Korean War was more of a war than today's wars, which are much closer, in my mind, to the definition of a police action.

My grandfather spoke very little about his time fighting in the Korean War. The few stories he did tell sounded much more like war than anything I experienced on my three deployments. Today's wars are much closer to police actions; on my last deployment, I had to wear a patch that read "ISAF," which stands for International Security Assistance Force. My comparison is that I used to give my old worn boots to the locals who needed them; our veterans who served in the Korean War sometimes had to get theirs off the dead to keep their feet warm. If Congress would have declared war, I don't believe anyone would have ever considered the Korean War to be just a "police action."

Progressing from the Korean War and the forgotten soldiers who fought there, things got even worse for those who served in Vietnam. The Vietnam War was very unpopular, resulting in many protests against it. The programs to help them return to civilian life remained largely unchanged from previous wars. Veterans would often return home by themselves, not as a unit. It was also not uncommon for a soldier to be in Vietnam one day and back in his hometown in less than forty-eight hours. Upon arriving home, many returning veterans were met by angry mobs blaming them for the war. They often felt they had to hide that they were veterans. Because of all the trouble the Vietnam veterans experienced, they make up almost half of the population of homeless veterans today.

The history of what it was like for veterans returning home from war is very important, because even though the wars and experiences are different for every soldier, what it is like to come home is largely the same. The history of veterans has been continually repeating itself. Today's war in Afghanistan has been going on longer than any other war we have been involved in. The war also doesn't seem to change civilians' lives very much compared to other wars. This makes the war different in that it can be easy to forget that we are even at war.

In the past, many people have either been pro-war and pro-troops or just completely against both, like in Vietnam. Today, many people have a mix of these opinions. They often say that they are against the war but support the troops. This is kind of strange, and it feels like they are slapping me in the face with one hand and patting me on the back to say thank you with the other. I know that's not what most people mean when they express this view. What I generally find people to mean by this is that they wish there wasn't war because it's a horrible thing, but that they also appreciate the men and women who volunteer to fight so they don't have to.

It's okay to be against war and support the troops, but it's also a thin line. A lot of people sacrificed a lot in the past two wars in Iraq and Afghanistan. Many sacrificed everything. If there is no reason to be there and the war is completely wrong, then all this was for nothing. So when you support the troops, you should also appreciate the sacrifices they made. Don't "thank the troops" simply because it's the politically correct thing to do.

When you walk through a military base, you don't find a bunch of soldiers talking about how badly they want a new war to start just so they can go live in a cruddy tent in the middle of nowhere and get shot at. What you do find, however, is that they are willing to do so if they are called upon, because they took an oath to defend freedom and liberty and are willing to take up arms to protect the ones they love. Soldiers of the past often felt the same, even those who served in Vietnam, who had their sacrifices rewarded with the repugnant label of "baby killer."

The changes a veteran experiences after coming home from war can be tough to cope with. While watching the

History Channel, I heard one man who was not named say, "Combat is going insane. It's asking normal kids to go out and kill people for twelve months. It's nuts. In order to do that you have to go insane for twelve months, you have to leave sanity." So when veterans get back from war, they are dealing with that and trying to come back to normal life. There are also dramatic changes in their lives, and along with that just about everyone gets a hearty scoop of culture shock to go with it.

I often hear many people say that coming home from a deployment is a lot like a new marriage. You start out in the "honeymoon" phase and then move on to a new phase where you have to work through the marital issues; you then either work through these issues or you don't. I've found that my experiences, as well as many of my friends', have been very similar to this. For most veterans, the first few weeks coming back from a deployment are usually pretty good or high-spirited because you're usually just happy to be home. Then you start to run into issues with your new life back home. This usually happens somewhere between a couple of weeks and a few months after getting back. I call this phase "the shock," and it can cause veterans to come under a great amount of stress. I call it the shock because it just kind of starts to hit veterans and then they just have to deal with it and let it pass through so that it can go away.

Many people deal with this in different ways. Many people going through the shock for the first time don't really have any clue what's going on, and it can make you think you're losing your mind. The first time I went through it, after my first deployment to Iraq, the stress caused my body to have physical side effects. It was tough. Fortunately, I did not have to endure this for very long; after only a couple of months, I was deployed to Afghanistan. Being deployed gives you almost a kind of careless stress that seems to counteract the shock.

Two months after I got home from my third deployment, I left the Army. Luckily for me, it was my third deployment, and I'd already built up my resilience to the shock. Resiliency is kind of like a muscle in the brain. If you work it out, you'll find it can get stronger over time. Unfortunately, many people get this brain muscle overstrained, and when your muscles are strained or torn they are hard to use. Being deployed can be like a constant strain on this muscle. I find the remedy that works for healing myself is often a simple answer: time. So to deal with the shock I find that if you know what's going on with it, you can just wait patiently because eventually the stress passes.

After leaving a career in the military, it can also be hard simply to find something else to do that is worthwhile. The challenges can be very similar to a civilian's experience when switching from one career to another. After large wars, it can be like the factory closing down in Flint, Michigan for veterans. Many soldiers become soldiers right out of high school and stay in for a long time, to the point that all they really know is soldiering, which can make it tough to figure out how to find a career as a civilian. With these changes, it is extremely important that there are programs out there to help veterans readjust, because a great deal of them need it in order to keep afloat after all they have sacrificed on behalf of everyone else.

As wars have changed over time, the struggles veterans have faced have remained largely unchanged. It is important that we remember those who serve and realize that without the sacrifices they've made, we would not have what we have today. It is important to continue to help them readjust and make it as civilians. When at war, soldiers do not leave each other behind. As a nation, we must strive to do the same.

WE DIDN'T UNDERSTAND

By Yvette M. Pino

On Tuesday, September 11, 2001, I was working as a props artisan and set builder for Goodspeed Musicals in Connecticut, not far from New York City. Because we did shows all weekend, Mondays and Tuesdays were our weekends, and the entire cast and much of the crew—my friends—were in the city on 9/11 going on auditions and checking in on their apartments. Luckily, no one from our theater was lost that day. It wouldn't be long, however, before I was gone.

I had decided to join the Army in order to get back into school and supplement my income. I was going to be a part-timer—one weekend a month, two weeks a year. Soon after 9/11, my recruiter called me, and I said, "No, I'm not interested anymore." I wasn't interested because I was scared. I didn't think I wanted to go to war. Then I started watching the news. I watched when we invaded Afghanistan and kicked out the Taliban, and it was at that time that I realized that if I wanted to have an informed opinion about what our country was going to do in response to global terrorism, I needed to be a part of it—a part of history. It was then that I decided to go active-duty.

What did I have to lose, really? It seemed like my job was a dead end. I was in a dead-end relationship. I wasn't making any forward progress in any part of my life. Plus, this was my generation's Pearl Harbor. This was the moment that would live in infamy. I knew that decades into the future, people would ask me, "Where were you on 9/11?" I wanted to be able to say that I was a part of it, that I was there and I answered the call. It was on 9/11 that we as a country had any sense of genuine care for one another.

It's been more than ten years since I went to Iraq for the first time. I feel sad when I think about how complacent we still all are. It's constantly in the back of my mind that the only thing that's going to wake us up again is another crazy disaster—another crazy, in-your-face moment. We're just so far removed from the terror we're fighting against. Most people just don't understand. They have no comprehension of what it's like to actually feel threatened.

At the same time, they don't understand for a second what it's like to be on the receiving end of America's military might. Those who have seen what America can do and actually know what it feels like to fight for your life come back with one of two mindsets. Some come back with a sometimes extreme sense of prejudice: "That's definitely the bad guy." Some come back with the idea that "I don't really know who the bad guys are—or were. I don't know why I was out there."

Most of us don't know what it's like to have our homes raided nearly every night by foreign invaders. Most of us don't know what it's like to be occupied by an invading force that doesn't trust you or even take the time to get to know you or try to understand you. Think about what would have happened had the Russians invaded us during the Cold War. Think about *Red Dawn*. Now let's say that we watched the news for months and saw newscast after newscast talking about how the Russians were eventually going to invade us—that they were going to depose our leaders and liberate us. Pretend that you know the Russians will invade, but you don't know when exactly or how.

I tried to explain this to my friends at Goodspeed when I came home on mid-tour leave from Iraq. I was trying to get them to see things from the Iraqi perspective. The Goodspeed Theater is on the Connecticut River, near the oldest swing bridge in the country. The only way to get across the river is on that swing bridge when it's open. I asked them to imagine seeing tanks and other military vehicles coming over the bridge to take over the theater. There's no fight happening, so you're not really sure what to think. They're supposed to be liberating you, right?

When the vehicles arrive, they make a perimeter around the theater because it's a perfect staging area for a Command Post (CP), mostly because it overlooks the river, has access to enough land for a small airstrip, has control over the swing bridge, and can therefore control traffic in and out of the small town of East Haddam, Connecticut. Perfect.

"What's a Command Post?" one person asked me.

"Wait, so Russian tanks are coming?" another asked incredulously.

Yes, and when they finish creating their perimeter, they kick all of you out of the theater and say, "We claim this as ours for the duration of our operation. You need to disperse. If we need you, we'll call you."

Then they come to your homes. After all, they need a place to house their troops. So they take over all of the houses surrounding the theater and kick all of the actors and actresses out. Sure, they'll offer you $200 for your house, thinking that they're helping out, but where are you supposed to find another place to stay long-term for $200?

Now you have no home, no place to work. You cannot cross the perimeter to go to places you used to be able to go. You cannot use the swing bridge unless you go through a convoy check or a patrol check. You no longer have a job, or a roof over your head, and you have to be off the streets by 10:00 p.m.

Then the raids begin.

They come into your dwelling, drag you out onto the street, and separate the men and the women. They may blindfold you and zip-tie your hands. Then they search your place for weapons of any sort. They're also looking for any kind of intelligence that may help them determine whether you're likely to take up arms against them.

Because you have no job and have nowhere else to go, you'll do anything to survive. At first, you might be willing to take on slave wages to help your new occupiers. After all, they need manual labor to rebuild the water treatment plant that they blew up during their invasion. They're willing to pay you a dollar per week to perform back-breaking labor. Your dollar a week gets paid to your foreman, who is as corrupt as they come, so you only really get a quarter a week. Good luck living and providing for your family on that. And if you get caught trying to take something, even a little bag of tea, you'll be fired and arrested. Maybe you'll end up dead. And you can guarantee that your dwelling will be added to a list to be searched routinely.

What would you do? You'd probably get pretty mad, right? Would you pick up a weapon? Plant a bomb?

It was at that point in my story that I found myself feeling really aggressive. My tone and posture had changed. My friends looked at me like they couldn't believe how much I had changed. I had lost my innocence, they thought. Some began to cry. I wanted them to think about what we were doing in their names. Some took what I said to heart. Others weren't ready to hear what I had to say. Maybe they're still not. I haven't kept in touch with most of them.

When I was in Iraq, I was told to treat them like dogs. Think about that. It's no wonder they fought back against our occupation. How long would it take you to fight back when you're forced to watch your wife and children man-handled every night? Watching your house get destroyed every night? Getting treated like a dog?

I see things differently now.

Most that haven't been overseas don't really care to see things differently. And when you tell them stories and try to give them a metaphorical scenario to think about—to show them what's really going on—they don't want to hear it.

"So you're sympathizing with the Iraqi people?" someone said to me once. "Yes, actually, I am."

Maybe my experiences affected how I looked at things. I wasn't kicking down doors, granted. I was working with 200 Iraqi men, cooking and preparing food, among other things, and I had a lot of conversations with them. Honestly, I'm embarrassed now about how naive I was back then—how little I knew or understood. One time, one of the men I was working with placed a map of Iraq in front of me and asked me to point out where we were at that moment. I couldn't do it.

We were told that they were primitive, ignorant, dirty, worthless, and backwards, but they taught me a lot I hadn't a clue about. For example, I'm from New Mexico, and it hit me one day how similar the Iraqi food was to the food I was used to eating back home. One day, I said, "Wow! Your guys' food tastes just like my food; it's weird. It's like I'm at home. I'm in the desert, your food tastes like my food, the environment looks like where I grew up."

One of them replied, "Yeah, it's because of the Spanish."

"I don't get it," I said. "I don't get how you're making that comparison."

"The Spanish invaded the Southwest in New Mexico," he said.

"Yeah. I know that. The conquistadors. I know that whole story," I replied.

"The Moors—and the Spanish—the Moors are Arab, and the Spanish..."

Then I had this thought—a moment of clarity: "I might actually be related to you. Maybe we share blood."

It was at that point that I started probing them about what they wanted from America. Here's what they told me: "We want our kids to go out and play. We want them to go out and play and not feel like they're going to get hurt. I want my kid to not be on the computer all day long. I want him to go outside and play. I want him to not be on computer games. I want my kids to go to school. I want my wife to be happy. I want…"

"That's what we want back home," I said.

"Why would it be so different?" he said. "Why would you think that what I want in my quality of life is so vastly different from yours?"

When I think about our occupation of Iraq, I realize now that we didn't understand the people. We didn't know what they believed or what they wanted. And now we're dealing with the disastrous results of that occupation. What would have happened if we had—even for a moment—thought about the people our decisions were affecting? I guess we'll never know.

SHARING THE COST OF WAR

By Travis Jochimsen

Throughout American History, veterans have not talked much about the events that unfolded for them while on the battlefield. It was a reminder of what they lost just for being a part of war. Whatever feelings they had were locked away and not talked about. They felt like they had to act like men. They feared that if they admitted to needing help, others would think you were weak.

My Uncle Fuzz, a Vietnam veteran, never talked about the experiences he had while serving his country. He was a closed book, to put it modestly. Maybe he resented the war because he was drafted, or maybe it was because he might have received the typical homecoming so many veterans of the Vietnam War were victims of. Whatever it was, the slightest mention of war would irritate him.

In 2006, I was lucky enough to be home in Wisconsin for the gun deer hunting season. After the day's hunt, a few members from neighboring hunting shacks stopped in to find out the details of the day's adventure. We all huddled around the table, engaged in conversation typical for deer camp—how someone saw a big buck but could not get a crack at him or how some flatlander from Illinois walked past somebody's tree stand and ruined their hunt.

During a short lull in the conversation, someone asked how my recent deployment in Iraq went. I answered his questions, most of which were the typical things civilians inquire about. Rick, a gentleman that owns land just down the road, interjected and spoke about how he thought Iraq was a waste of time and that we should get out of there. Heads nodded in affirmation of his comment, and Fuzz stepped in to say, "We're done talking about war in here, period! Go someplace else if you wanna talk about it!" The shack was silent for a brief moment before everyone began socializing about lighter topics.

I didn't care that he did not want Iraq to be the topic of discussion. Truth be told, I didn't want to talk about it either. Talking about chasing a monster buck was more suited for me. It did, however, make me curious about his service in the Army. I recalled some pictures on display at his home of him receiving a Combat Infantry Badge while in Vietnam. My interest was sparked!

Like veterans who have come before me, I haven't told many stories. This past year, however, I was asked to tell a story of my service to an artist who would then make a fine art print illustrating my story. Here's what I told him:

I was on my third deployment to Iraq from 2007 to 2009, and I was assigned to 3rd Brigade Combat Team, 4th Infantry Division. I was attached to my company's Military Police platoon, which had three missions: One squad would be a personal security detachment for the brigade's executive officer. Two squads would rotate between doing detainee backhaul and escorting different high-profile civilians—usually some higher-up from the U.S. Department of the Interior. The rest of the platoon would work at the detainee holding area, where detainees would be incarcerated until transferred. My squad was one of two that did detainee backhaul and what we later called "babysitting trips," where we provided security while civilians poked around Sadr City.

The day started off like any other. I went to the gym for an hour, got breakfast, took a shower, and headed to our company command post for sensitive items report, which was due at 0900. SSG Santos was already in the office waiting for me so we could drink some coffee and get ready for that night's mission. While we were filling out the paperwork, our LT walked in with news of a mission she had just received. This mission was pretty cool. Someone was going to fly down to a base in the southern part of the city and pick up a HVT (high-value target) that was taken prisoner during a mission the night before. The LT had been looking for us to find out who was going to go pick this guy up, since detainee backhaul was our squad's responsibility at the time.

Santos and the LT talked about it for a few minutes while I went out to smoke. Before I could finish, they walked out to tell me I had been chosen to go because I was good at the paperwork. They informed me that I needed to find someone to go with me because another mission was going to happen at the same time and our squad could not give up any more personnel.

I walked down to the motor pool to see if I could get my friend, Mike Milsap, to go with me. I explained what we were going to be doing to his superiors, and they agreed to let him help me out. The mission was simple: get on a Blackhawk and fly down to the COP (combat outpost) to pick this guy up, have him checked out by a medic to ensure that he did not have any bruises or other injuries (if he did have any, I would need to annotate before I signed for him), go over his personal belongings, and check to make sure that the paperwork was filled out correctly. We also had to look over the rest of his detainee packet to ensure that all signatures were present and nothing was missing.

I packed my assault bag with extra flex cuffs and a pair of protective eye goggles that had been taped over, and I stuffed in a vest for our detainee to wear. I was given a cell phone and a leather folding ID badge with contents that would ensure we got our seats on the helicopter. We drove down to the flight line where we waited until the next pair of Blackhawks arrived to pick up passengers.

When we arrived, I showed the civilian contractor at the flight line window the contents of the leather badge and explained to him that we would be getting on the first pair of birds out of Taji. Once we boarded our ride, we began our trip south, stopping at every combat outpost on the way. When we arrived at our destination, we were greeted by someone who was going to take us to start the process of turning this detainee over to us. When they brought the detainee into the room to be checked out, I couldn't help but notice how small of a man he was. He was probably only sixty-four inches tall and weighed 140 pounds. It was hard to look at this man as someone who was responsible for the deaths of many of my brothers and sisters. He looked far too weak to be capable of that.

The man who stood before me was the head of a large cell group. He was an "ace card," which meant that he was at the top of the most-wanted list. He was a bad dude who led a group that would place IEDs and EFPs (explosively formed projectiles) throughout the Baghdad area. They also supplied weapons and munitions for attacks against U.S. and Iraqi forces. I'm sure there was more in his file, but I just glanced over it. What was more important was making sure his detainee packet had everything inside it and that it was correct so he wouldn't accidentally be released.

When he looked at everyone who was standing in the room, you could almost feel his hate for us radiate from his stare. When he looked at me, all I could do was look back at him and crack a smile. The reason I smiled at him was because he was done killing my fellow soldiers. For once we had won, and it felt good.

Once the transfer was complete, we headed back to the flight line for our flight back. We put body armor on him and placed the taped-over goggles on his eyes. After a 15-minute wait, we could start to hear the sound of rotors in the distance as our ride got closer. When the Blackhawks started to land, the detainee, who I was holding onto by the back of his bicep, began to shake. He then tried to sit on the ground as if he was trying to let me know he was not going to make this trip with us. Mike and I got him up on his feet, and we walked him to the helicopter. The detainee was doing everything he could to make this as hard for us as possible. It reminded me of young kid throwing a temper tantrum.

I'm sure he was scared out of his mind—rightly so, considering he was in the hands of his enemy. That was probably a ride he never forgot. Once we got him inside the bird, we placed him in a seat and fastened the five-point harness around him securely. As we flew back, I just looked out over the countryside, and for the first time I felt like I had done something worthwhile while deployed. It is something that I will never forget.

When I came home on leave from that tour to Iraq, Fuzz asked if I would help him plant soybeans out at the hunting shack. I agreed to help him, and halfway through planting the field, he stopped the tractor and said, "Let's go have a treat!" While we were enjoying our drink, I asked him about the Army chow in Vietnam. He laughed and said, "Not good!" I figured since he entertained my first question, I might as well ask him another. Without hesitating, I said, "Hey Fuzz, what unit were you in?" He paused a second, and replied "1/77 Air Cavalry. Now talk about something else!" Despite his displeasure in the conversation, he also told me that he operated an M60 machine gun during his tour.

After that day I never asked him another question. We both had an unspoken agreement to leave the topic alone.

After growing up around Fuzz, hearing stories of how nervous going in the woods before daylight made him, I saw firsthand what "bottling it up" can do to a person. Fuzz made that work somehow, and he was someone I admired and loved very much. Maybe that old stigma that tells a man he can't talk about his feelings is gone in today's culture—maybe it's not. I believe that if sharing your experiences can somehow help you move past the costs of going to war for your country, you should do it.

MY FIRST MISSION

By Ryan Callahan

Over the last 10 years of my life I like to believe that I have matured in many ways. Most of the credit for my maturity belongs to the United States military. There were times I hated being in the Army and many times I regretted that I joined, but looking back now I realize that I would do it all over again. Without hesitation.

I was still in high school when I signed up, but I was old enough to know exactly what I wanted to do with my service. I wanted to be in the infantry. Just like most guys, I didn't listen to any advice my peers or parents gave me: "You will regret it!" they said. "Get a job that will help you transition back into civilian life," they suggested. My personal favorite was, "You're stupid; you know it will suck, right?" I didn't listen though. Young men rarely do.

This is all so funny to me now, considering that recently an old friend of mine talked to me about joining the military. He told me he was thinking about joining the infantry so that he could better support his family. He was lying to himself. No one joins the infantry for their families. They do it for themselves. In fact, I can name a hundred other jobs in the Army that would be much better suited for someone who wants to support his family. I gave him the same advice and suggestions I got when I decided to enlist: "Get a job that will help you transition back into civilian life." I knew I was wasting my breath. If he is anything like most infantry guys, it won't matter what I tell him.

On my first deployment to Afghanistan, I was an assistant gunner for an M240 Bravo machine gun team. We were on a smaller post in the northeastern part of Afghanistan from October 2010 through February 2011. It was very mountainous and cold there. Our rooms were in an old Afghan building, but they were refurnished for the military to use. Our squad shared one open room with bunk beds. After a few days, we started building our own little huts, using blankets and the bunk beds inside the room. We placed our huts along the walls of the room and in the middle we had a couch set up with a TV to entertain us. Looking back now, I realize that it was actually one of the nicest places I stayed in during my time overseas. We didn't have any problems with our heater, and there was even a little privacy in the huts that we built. The food was actually pretty good, too, since the chow hall where we ate was funded by the Navy. The only problem that I remember with the post was that because I was a private, I had to fill up the water tanks on the roof of the building every morning so that the bathroom would have running water. It was during that deployment that one of the most memorable events of my military service happened.

It was some time during November. I was sitting in my little cave. My team leader came into the room and told me that we might be going out that night. He told me that the 101st Airborne requested our help. They were getting pretty beat up and needed us to keep the Taliban busy while they regrouped and took care of their casualties. They were being held up in Kunar Province, up in the mountains. No one ever heard or really knew much about the majority of the missions we went on. After a while, it became really difficult to remember the particulars of each mission. They came one after another after another. A blur. This mission was different, though. It was my first, and it was the first and only time in my military career that my unit was asked for help. This was the type of mission that had more meaning to us. It was very exciting. I remember going to the ready-room, where we had all our equipment set up. My kit was in the far back corner, sitting on its shelf. I ran through my checklist, making sure I had water in my

CamelBak, my ammo was clean, all my magazines were loaded up, my weapon was oiled and clean, and that the laser on it worked.

For that particular mission, I remember packing about 500 rounds of ammunition (more than usual) into my assistant gunner bag, which also contained the machinegun tripod, extra barrels, a sleeping bag, and some snacks. I was excited about the rounds we were bringing with us. They were infrared tracers, with a mix of armor-piercing rounds. I could tell by the purple and black tips. After I got all of my gear strapped on, we had to weigh ourselves to make sure we didn't weigh too much for the Chinook helicopter to take off with us inside. That day I weighed in at 315 pounds.

After we had our plan all set, we started to kit up and head outside for roll call. We were ready to go, but someone from the tactical operations center (TOC) told us that one of the Chinooks was broken. I don't know what was wrong with it, but I consider myself lucky that day. I found out later from my team leader that the place we would have gone that night was overrun by around forty armed Afghans. It would have just been three of us up there if the mission had gone off without a hitch.

The next day, we knew we were going out. The Chinook was fixed. We went through the same ritual as the day before. Right before we started our roll call, a chaplain came out and asked to pray with us. I thought it was funny, because usually I expected an uplifting and encouraging prayer or speech. Instead, he started praying about how dangerous this mission actually was and how some of us might not come back. I remember thinking to myself, "Wow, thanks, that's encouraging."

After his little prayer, we loaded on our buses, which took us to the airfield where the Chinooks were already running. I remember lining up behind it. I could feel the heat from the exhaust and hear the loud rotors. I could feel the power in my chest. While the leaders recounted the numbers and made sure they had everyone, I made sure all my stuff was right. I always checked. Then we started loading into the Chinook. The seats lined the walls on each side. I decided to sit in the middle facing the ramp. I remember looking to my left and seeing one of the Gatling gunners checking his weapon.

It wasn't long before we took off. After a while, we got the ten-minute out sign. Again I checked all my stuff. Then the six-minute sign came. I turned on my night-vision goggles and checked the laser on my rifle. Then the three-minute call came, and those of us sitting on the floor got up on one knee and finished getting ready. Then came the one-minute call. We were almost there.

As the Chinook started lowering its ramp and touching down, I grabbed my safety lanyard with my right hand and unbuckled it. We all ran off into the Afghan darkness. I couldn't see anything from the brownout; there was so much dirt in the air. Rocks were hitting me from behind. Then the training kicked in. We got into a half-moon formation and kneeled down. As soon as everybody was off the Chinook, it took off, leaving us to our task. Then everything got quiet. The squad and team leaders got their radio checks, and we started to get into our order of movement.

We had landed in a dry field. I could see a very high mountain to the left of me. We eventually made our way to that mountain, which was covered in vegetation. This was the first time I saw trees and a forest in Afghanistan. The mountain we climbed was steep. I remember having to grab branches to pull myself up the slope. It took us a while to reach the top. This was the spot where the forty fighters had been the day before. This time, however, there was nothing.

The sun started to come up, and we started walking toward a village that was located down inside a valley. This village was extremely isolated. My job was to provide security while the line squads started clearing the houses. We were a mobile gun team, a very heavy mobile gun team. As the line squads cleared the houses, my gun team would relocate to keep up with them. This meant I was walking up and down mountains all day long. Throughout the entire day, all I could hear were explosions from the ordnances that were dropped. That day, I heard more bombs and mortars explode than on any other days combined.

After we cleared the village and things started to quiet down a little, we set in. We bunkered ourselves into a building we cleared and set up our security. I was lying on the roof of the building we took. It was flat; there was no cover on the roof, but I could see over the entire valley. I remember my squad leader telling me to stay down because there was a sniper out there—somewhere. This was great, because I was completely in the open, with no cover around me, behind a machine gun. We ended up grabbing a huge piece of lumber and putting it in front of us. As long as we lay in the prone we were fine.

Most of the bombs dropped that day were danger close, meaning that they were dropped within 600 meters of our location. My squad leader came up to me and told us to stay down, that they were going to drop two 1,000-pound bombs very close to us. In the movies, the bombs always sound like a whistle, but they are loud when they are close. They are very loud. It's like there is a person screaming in your ear. I remember feeling the shockwave from the blast. During the two days we were on that mission, we dropped multiple 500-pound bombs, those two 1,000-pound bombs, 105s, multiple hell fires, and we did a lot of gun runs.

After they dropped the two bombs, I ate my lunch. My squad leader called me to him, and we sat there eating our MREs (meals ready to eat). The rest of the day was quiet, except for the occasional gun run. Once the sun started to set, we decided to leave. The 101st had done what they needed to do, so we started moving back up the mountain very slowly. Everything hurt when we walked up the mountain. I remember my legs starting to cramp up and my shoulders hurting from the weight of the assistant gunner bag.

Once we made it back to the helicopter landing zone and set up security, we waited for the night. It was one of the coldest nights that I remember in Afghanistan. My squad leader was with my gun team, and one of us would try to sleep while the other two would pull security. While I was on security, I felt so exhausted that I started seeing things on the side of the mountain. I knew my eyes were messing with me, but it was still distressing.

Eventually the Chinook returned to take us home. Leaving on that bird was an indescribably amazing feeling. I had survived my first mission. We had accomplished what we had set out to accomplish. Now we could rest.

All told, our mission resulted in an estimated seventy-five enemy fighters killed in action. We lost one that day and had another three injured.

That mission and others like it have changed me. After doing this type of work, I've learned to appreciate the small things. I don't complain about schoolwork or about my new job. I don't complain because at least now I don't have to sleep outside in the cold, or work for over twenty-four hours—or have to worry about being shot or blown up. I can look back and tell myself that it could always be worse.

A LIFE OF CHANGE

By Matt Fortun

May 29, 2010 was graduation day, and my emotions couldn't have been any more confused. Graduation day is supposed to be an exciting day for high school seniors as they embrace the end of their high school years and prepare for college. This was not the case for me. My feelings were actually quite the opposite. Yes, I was excited to graduate, but nobody knew the fear that consumed me on the inside—the fear of the unknown. Like most graduates, the fear of what to expect in college would settle in eventually, but that would normally occur at the end of summer break. I, on the other hand, had only two weeks until I walked into the unknown. College is the normal thing to pursue after high school, but I did not choose to take that path. Instead, I chose to alter my life in an entirely different way, by enlisting in the military. With graduation now complete, I was about to travel into unfamiliar territory.

Before I left for the Army, I knew I had to take advantage of the time I had at home with family and friends. With each passing day, it seemed as though I didn't have enough time to do everything I wanted to. Two days before I left, my friends invited me out bowling. As we approached the bowling alley, I noticed familiar vehicles in the parking lot. Then as we entered, I was given a very warm welcome. It turned out that my friends and family set up a surprise going-away party for me. This was the best surprise anyone had ever given me. Without the surprise going-away party, I think my transition into the military would have been a lot worse.

On June 13, I left home with the mindset of not knowing when I would be back. I embarked on my journey to better myself and serve my country. After several flights,

I had arrived for basic training at Fort Jackson, South Carolina. I spent my first few days in reception, where I was issued uniforms and learned basic marching drills. After the few days spent at reception, I boarded the bus that transported me to my unit. Upon arrival to my destination, a drill sergeant entered the bus and began shouting orders to get my ass off his bus. One by one the bus emptied and we sprinted to a designated location. As I reached the designated area, the drill sergeants ordered me into the push up position. For the next twenty minutes I was forced to do exercises while being welcomed to my unit.

Basic training lasted for ten weeks. These ten weeks were the longest weeks of my life. Never before have I been pushed as hard as the drill sergeants pushed me. Over the course of the ten weeks, basic training covered several training requirements, with marksmanship, physical training, and survival skills leading the charge. Before the military, I never knew my physical and mental limitations. I had thought some high school classes were difficult, but what I had to endure though basic training was way more difficult. In order for me to pass basic training, I had to forget about everything that was going on back home and focus on the task at hand. Of course, it was easier said than done to stop thinking about the life I had left back home. The thought of my family and friends was the biggest motivation in my completion of basic training. Without the ability to write letters and make occasional phone calls back home, I think I would have gone crazy. When I was not able to communicate with ease, the stress and sadness took control.

Once I graduated, I was notified of my next training location, which was Fort Belvoir, Virginia. Out of my entire company, I was the only person going to Fort Belvoir. I was once again moving across the country without anyone else. As I left basic training to go to my advanced individual training, or AIT, as it's called, the nervous feelings and the fear of the unknown regained control of my body. My drill sergeants from basic training informed me that AIT would be somewhat like basic training but that we would have weekends off. I was so excited to know that I could once again enjoy weekends and wear civilian clothing. The freedoms I had prior to basic training were finally coming back to me.

Fort Belvoir was a great place to be stationed due to its close proximity to Washington, D.C. Every weekend that I was eligible to leave post, I went wandering around the D.C. area. The reason I was stationed at Fort Belvoir was for my training to become a geospatial engineer. The job of a geospatial engineer is to create map products that provide imagery and detailed information about a specific location's terrain features. The maps would be requested by helicopter pilots, infantrymen, and just about anyone who would go on a mission, whether it was a training mission or a mission in combat. These maps were critical to mission success. My AIT training meant putting all my focus on this one job to ensure I obtained the proper skills to manage the workload and responsibility that came with it. Each day of training began at 8:00 a.m. and lasted until approximately 5:00 p.m. At that time, I would get on the bus to go get dinner. Dinner was the last task of the day on most days, but there were some days that required extra time on the computer systems to finish a specific product. There was such a large amount of time required on the computer systems that I actually had to take mandatory ten-minute breaks to relax my mind. With each day that passed, the pressure to complete my products increased tremendously. I accomplished each product in a timely manner, but over time, it became more and more difficult to understand exactly what the hell I was doing. My performance in the class wasn't top notch, but I managed to exceed the requirements for graduation in my field of training.

My AIT lasted from September 2010 until February 2011. As Christmas approached, I was informed that all of us soldiers had to leave for the holiday season. I was so thrilled to hear this, as it was my opportunity to go home for the first time in six months. I could barely contain myself in my seat after takeoff because of the excitement I felt about going home. The look on my dad's face as I walked out of the arrival gate was priceless. He knew it had been six months and that I was a changed man. The next two weeks spent at home with family and friends were the best two weeks I had ever had up until that point. My family and friends gave me the warmest of welcomes, and we then spent great quality time together—memories I will never forget.

Just as I seemed to get comfortable and readjusted to being back home, I had to leave to go back to Fort Belvoir. During my last thirty days of AIT training, I was informed of the duty station I would report to after graduation. My papers read "12th Combat Aviation Brigade; Ansbach, Germany." My mind could not grasp the concept of finally going to my first duty assignment, let alone going to my first duty assignment overseas. I was shocked, but kind of excited at the same time. At no point in time did I ever think I would get a chance to travel to Europe. With all the challenges I already had to endure up to this point in my military career, this was by far the most challenging. Immediately after receiving my orders to Germany, I informed my family and friends. The hardest thing about telling them I was going to Germany was the fact that I would not know when I would be back. Now, preparing to increase the distance between my family and my friends by about 5,000 miles more, I knew it would be more difficult to return home.

On February 11, 2011, I graduated from AIT. Just like after basic training, I was about to embark on my next journey alone. Several of my classmates were sent to South Korea and various bases in the United States. I was the only one heading to Germany. As exciting as it sounds to be going to Germany, going alone was not how I imagined it. Following our graduation ceremony, our platoon sergeants took my entire class to the Ronald Reagan International Airport for departure to our duty stations.

On February 12, 2011, I arrived at the Frankfurt International Airport in Germany after approximately fourteen hours of total travel time. Due to my recent travels across the United States, I had grown accustomed to navigating the airports; however, this was not the United States anymore. Luckily for me, the signs had enough information in English that I was able to find my way to the arrival gate.

It was a three-hour bus ride from the airport to my duty station. When I arrived, I met two sergeants who were to be my supervisors. I was lucky; I couldn't have asked for nicer people. These two showed a tremendous amount of respect and went above and beyond expectations to help me settle in to my new "home."

Throughout 2011, I was able to make many friends and enjoy my time out around Germany. But, as the end of 2011 approached, the biggest test of my life would be announced, the test of deployment. I knew a deployment to Afghanistan would most likely happen, but I did not expect it to happen so soon. With deployment looming, my mind began to think of the worst things that could happen, and my heart began to beat faster than ever before. Most twenty-year-olds would be in college or working to prepare for college, but that was not my situation. I would have never thought of being deployed to Afghanistan at the age of twenty, but that was exactly what was about to happen. I was already 5,000 miles away from home, and now the Army was about to take me a few thousand more. With deployment came a lot of preparation and training to ensure the mission would be accomplished safely and successfully.

In October 2011, our unit commenced a three-week field training exercise which was to indicate what would be expected from every section during deployment. The training that took place during those three weeks focused on how well we worked together. Each section provided different skills and knowledge to apply to the overall mission. My job was to provide map products to the helicopter pilots who commenced the practice medical evacuation missions. The other sections provided Internet capability, phone and radio connection, and accountability of personnel and equipment. The three weeks spent at this training exercise were long and exhausting. We all knew what was at stake and completed the training exercise safely and effectively. The knowledge gained from the training exercise would prove key to the success of our deployment. The end of the training exercise brought the end of 2011, which meant deployment was less than five months away.

March 2012 came upon us, and our unit was given the go-ahead to take leave, go home, and visit family for two weeks. Each individual who opted to take advantage of this opportunity was designated a certain two-week period they could leave. Not having been in the military a full two years, I was about to go home for the third time. Once again, the time home would give me a new boost of confidence and would allow me to get my mind set on the deployment. After another amazing two weeks at home with family and friends, I returned to Germany with only one month until my departure for Afghanistan. In addition to work and everything else I had going on, the last month before deployment consisted of packing, receiving required medical shots, and saying goodbye to those staying behind. It was a hectic month, but it was all part of being in the Army. Up until this time, my rank in the army was a Private First Class. The day before departure I was promoted from

Private First Class to Specialist. With the promotion came higher expectations and more responsibility.

On May 4, 2012, our unit departed the base for the airport. For the next day or two, our time would be spent traveling from Germany to Afghanistan with a few stops in between. Upon arrival in Afghanistan, I realized it wasn't as bad as I thought, because we were located in northern Afghanistan, where very few attacks occurred. Knowing we were in a safe location compared to other bases in Afghanistan was a relief to me and my family. Deploying to fight for our country is part of the job, but my heart and mind were not ready for that big of a task. Of course, with time spent in country, my brain engaged in a rhythm to help me survive, succeed, and excel at the task of deployment.

From the day I arrived until the day I left, I worked twelve-hour night shifts from 8 p.m. to 8 a.m. Because of my shift, I would sleep from about 9:30 a.m. to 6:30 p.m., skip eating dinner, and only eat at about 2 a.m. The need for sleep in order to function properly during my shift took priority over the need to eat. As I was able to snack at work, I figured I didn't need to eat when I could sleep. My shifts were never really exciting, but they were very productive. Almost every night, my shop would receive a request for terrain analysis for a certain location. I collected the information from the request and compiled it into a useful product.

As my days continued in Afghanistan, I found myself in a situation that gave me much to rejoice. One morning after a long night of work, my platoon sergeant approached me with a stack of papers. With these papers, he told me to begin out-processing with the unit and start packing my things, as I was heading back to Germany. I was so confused about why I was leaving to go back so soon. As it turned out, our shop was informed that one soldier must be sent back with the group that was already set to leave. Working in my shop were my three sergeants and myself. One of my staff sergeants was platoon sergeant, another staff sergeant was in charge of the urinalysis, and my sergeant needed this deployment to help earn his promotion. Because of the positions held by my sergeants, I was the obvious choice to leave. I was scheduled to leave Afghanistan sometime during the final week of June 2012. My deployment was cut well short of what I expected, but I was so glad to know I was about to leave the hellhole known as Afghanistan. The day before I left, I was given the opportunity to go to the range and qualify with a few of the German weapon systems. I spent half a day at the range waiting to qualify, and by the end of it, I had qualified with a bronze medal. I may not have qualified with gold, but bronze was still good enough to have earned me the right to wear the medal on my dress uniform.

On June 28, 2012, I was on a plane heading back to Germany. Although my deployment was cut short, I still played a role in the success of our mission. If I had not left Afghanistan when I did, I would have missed out on so many of the friendships I made shortly after I returned to Germany. During my weekends, I started going out with a few of the people I met, and we started going to the Irish pub right in town. We would have never guessed that one trip to the Irish pub would lead to a weekly hangout.

With our weekly visits to the Irish pub, I was able to meet a lot of really cool people and become friends with many of them. The pub started hosting different events on the weekends, and one of them was karaoke. Karaoke night was held once a month, and it quickly became an event I enjoyed. For the next couple months, I spent my weekends at the pub with my friends and spent my weekdays working with the military intelligence analysts that were part of the rear detachment. I had to work with the military intelligence analysts because my topographic section was still in Afghanistan, so I had no equipment to utilize. My first supervisor returned from Afghanistan at the end of August, followed by the rest of my unit in September. My entire company was only deployed for four months, as we were part of the procedure to draw down soldiers from Afghanistan. After my shop's return from Afghanistan, the daily tasks were brought down to a minimum and every day seemed to pass with ease.

I requested to go home for Christmas of 2012, because it had been nine months since I was last home, which was the longest I had ever been away in my entire life. With each time I returned, the welcome or acknowledgment from others got less and less noteworthy. I want to believe that it got lower because they assumed I would be home at some point. Although I never saw any combat during my deployment, how could my friends and family have been so sure I would return home at all? I am glad that they had optimism and positive thoughts about my deployment, but to treat me like I was never in any danger was kind of ridiculous. I didn't want to be praised or rewarded for making it through my deployment; I just wanted people to understand the possibility of my not returning. With each return, my friends would talk to me less and less, and it just irritated me that such long-time good friends could just up and walk out on me at times I needed them the most. After my two weeks home, I realized that the longer I spent in the military, the more friends of mine would distance themselves from me. I knew at that moment that I would complete my contract with the military and then get out as a civilian.

I made many friends in Germany, but at the time I didn't think they would be able to replace the relationships I had established with everyone back home. My friends back home had been in my life for five or more years at that point, while my friends in Germany had only been in my life for about two years. People say the friends you make in the military end up being the closest friends in life. I eventually began to realize that was true. And once I got over the fact that I wasn't back home, I started to spend more time with my friends in Germany, and I stopped worrying so much about those back home. If my friends back home wanted to stay in my life, they would at least attempt to do so. I ended up spending 2013 completely focused on making myself happy and not thinking of things back home. Throughout 2013, my weekends were spent with friends, drinking, going out, and singing karaoke. At this point in time, karaoke night turned into karaoke weekend. I had finally learned to stop caring about what people thought of me, and I started doing what was best for me.

From October 28 to November 21, I attended the Warrior Leadership Course. Upon successful completion of the course and approval from a promotion board, I would be eligible for a promotion to sergeant. During the first weekend of the course, I spent many hours at the warrior zone, which is a place for single soldiers to relax and use the free Wi-Fi. While at the warrior zone, I contacted my dad and had him purchase a car I was interested in. Meanwhile, on the same night, I also purchased a plane ticket home to Wisconsin for three weeks in December. The course seemed to take forever, but I managed to successfully graduate and made my shop proud. With the completion of the leadership course, I was able to shift my focus to the next big transition of my life, the transition out of the military. With June 2014 right around the corner, I started to think about how life would change yet again as I prepared to leave the military after four years. I was beyond ready to leave the military. I missed being able to make decisions on my own terms.

I spent December 16 to January 5 at home in Wisconsin. My visit home was just like any other time, except I had three weeks to enjoy my time. Nothing out of the ordinary happened, except the final night. On my last night, I met up with a few of my high school classmates and went bowling. At the bowling alley, I was able to see one of my classmates I had not seen since high school graduation in May 2010. We were pretty excited to catch up on lost time. After an hour or so of bowling, we headed back to town and went drinking at the bar. We had several drinks and then they decided to call it a night. I decided to stay and had a few more beers before leaving for the airport the next morning. I drank until about 1 a.m. and then walked back to my house to get some sleep, as I had to be up by 6 a.m. After I left to fly back to Germany for the last time, I was so excited to know that my time in the military had finally reached the end.

From January until April, my mind was focused on getting out of the military. As soon as April hit, I began the out-processing procedure from the military. May 2 was the last night I spent at the Irish pub, and I was very sad to know I would not return anytime soon. My friends insisted that because it was my last night at the pub, I sing one last song with them for karaoke. We decided to sing "What Is Love" by Haddaway. After the night concluded, I had so many mixed feelings running through me as I got ready to leave Germany and the military. I knew that while I was excited to leave the Army, I was sad to have to leave my friends.

May 9, 2014 was the day I left the military to enter back into the civilian world. Many things had changed since I enlisted, but it was all to make me the man I am today. The mixed emotions had consumed my body, and I was confused about how I should feel. I knew I should feel excited to begin civilian life again, but then I knew I should feel nervous to begin life outside of the military. On this day, I had to say goodbye to all the friends I had made along the way and say goodbye to the place I had called home for the last three and a half years. When I left, it was just like all my other military travels: I traveled alone. My military career was short but well-lived. It was time to move on to life outside of the military and begin life as a college student. Throughout my years in the military, I learned to overcome and adapt to new experiences on short notice. Leaving the military was one of those things I adapted to rather quickly, and I felt like I had never even left the civilian life.

Leaving the civilian life to enlist in the military was the best decision I ever made. The experience of the military taught me things I could never learn as a civilian and gave me a whole new perspective on life. Without the military, I would not be who I am today, would not have been able to travel the world, and would not be able to pay for college. If I had to do things all over again, I would do it all the same, but with a few minor changes. Exactly like when I first enlisted in the military, life after the military is another journey into the unknown. I had a good idea of what I wanted to pursue in the civilian life, but I also knew I would hit a few bumps along the way. My feelings for the military are nothing but great, as it provided me the opportunity to serve my country and gave me the resources to succeed. If there is one piece of advice I would give to others about life, it is to be ready for change. Change allowed me to see that there is a whole world out there, full of experiences. Change brought me closer to family and friends. Change gave me the resources to succeed in the military and in the civilian life. Change is a good thing. Change is life.

NOT EVERYONE WHO COMES HOME IS HOME

By Tyler Pozolinski

Alone. Alienated. Abandoned. Your eyes scan the battle-field. The sun ricochets off the sand, blinding you, forcing you to look away. The air hangs heavy, pulling your shoulders down. The smell burns itself into your memory. You'll never forget. Then there are the sounds–men screaming out in pain and fear. But what you hear doesn't register. It's like a foreign language. Then you find yourself standing outside yourself. Death hangs over you. It surrounds you. Faster than an Olympic sprinter, your heart feels as if it's going to punch out of your chest, and just when it becomes too much, you wake up only to realize you've already lived this before. You don't know it when it's happening to you, but you will never be the same. This war is your war, and it has forever changed you.

We don't realize how much our lives change and form every day. Experiences like these are constantly shaping and guiding our lives, ultimately determining who we are in the end. We can't choose what we will experience in our lives, but we can determine how we face it and interpret it. I am a veteran, and my experiences have forever changed who I am and how I see the world.

To this day, one dream returns to me. It has changed me, rocking me to my core. It is midday in a strange land, and the sun pulls the sweat out of my body. I'm standing in what used to be a village. It might have been there for hundreds of years, but today it lies in ruins. Filled with a thick miasma that poisons the soul, I look around to confirm what my nose has already told me–death is all around. Once you've smelled that smell, you never forget it. I stand in awe of this village, which now looks more like a graveyard, filled with dead enemies. I'm looking around for my brothers, only to realize I stand alone in this destruction. I alone am responsible for the outcome of this battle.

Then everything changes. The battlefield is gone, and I am alone in a dark world with a single street light beating down on me. I find myself hunched over with my head tucked between my knees, alone and unable to see what lies before me. Familiar faces begin to float around me, muttering their hateful spew. I can understand what they're saying to me. "You're a freak," they yell. "Who do you think you are?" they ask. "You don't belong with the rest of us!" The figures fade, and a light burns away everything. I wake up confused, angry, and disoriented, asking, *What does this mean? Why do I keep having this dream?* Before I can find the answer, the dream returns, a constant reminder of the person I have been molded into.

Not all combat veterans have dreams like this. There was a time that I actually looked forward to having them, as if being haunted by dreams would somehow validate what I had been through. I could point to my dreams as proof that I had been there, that I had been in the worst place in the world–and survived. For generations, combat veterans have relived their experiences in their dreams only to wake up in a cold sweat, lost, confused, and wondering what just happened. Dreams have a way of pulling us away and showing us things we sometimes don't want to see or things that we are trying to forget. Other times, dreams can convey a deeper meaning.

The veteran's road to recovery is oftentimes filled with lots of pain. Sometimes we don't ever fully come back from it. The crucibles we survive not only define us—they forever change us. We look in the mirror, and we don't recognize what we see. To this day, I find myself struggling to answer the question every veteran struggles to answer: "Who have I become?"

My dreams are collections of memories that have been burned into my brain, like a hot brand to the skin. The scar the brand leaves might eventually heal, but it will always be there, whether I like it or not. Trying to avoid such dreams is like staring at your shadow, hoping it will go away. That's why I don't try anymore. My dreams stand testament to the crucible I have endured. I kind of like my dreams.

IN SICKNESS AND IN HEALTH

By Kyle Nowak

When most people think of war, they tend to picture combat and enemy engagements as the biggest threat. What most people forget—or maybe never even realized—is that disease has long been the biggest killer on the battlefield. Two-thirds of all soldiers who died during the American Civil War were not felled by bullet or bayonet—they died from disease. Things haven't improved all that much in the past 150 years. Our soldiers are still getting sick, and many of them are dying. Sometimes, we don't even exactly know why.

Ever since I was in kindergarten, I have been involved in sports and lived an active lifestyle. Growing up, I wrestled and played basketball, and in sixth grade, I started lifting weights. When high school came around, I was a part of four state-champion football teams, and I went to state four years in a row for discus throw in track and field. I took third place at state one year and followed that up with a gold medal the following year. As much as I was dedicated and loved my sports, there was one thing I loved doing more than anything, and that was lifting weights. I loved every little bit of weightlifting: spending time with my friends and brothers, setting goals, preparing for sports, challenging myself, and pushing my body to its limits.

When it came time to graduate from high school, I joined the Army, even though I had many offers from colleges for sports. I turned those down so I could serve in the infantry. I wanted to be in the infantry because I have always loved doing things that were physically demanding. I also thought that if I served in the infantry, I would be doing my part in protecting our country's freedom.

Infantry School was pretty much what I expected. Both the physical and mental aspects were a breeze, because I came from multiple sports in high school that pushed me way harder mentally and physically. The biggest challenge I faced was learning how to deal with people who did not have the same drive or motivation that I was always used to being around. I actually really enjoyed Infantry School and was pretty excited about my choice to join.

Directly following Infantry School, I was shipped to the other side of Fort Benning for Airborne School. This was by far the most enjoyable school I attended while I was in the military. It is one of the only things I am actually proud of during my time in. Airborne School was beyond easy, but getting to jump out of airplanes was something I never thought I would do, and it was just an overall fun time. Upon graduation, I was so motivated to get to my unit and meet the people I was going to be working with.

Arriving at my unit was a rude awakening and an extreme eye-opener to the outside world beyond my hometown of Stratford, Wisconsin. I was suddenly surrounded by drugs, bad leadership, and an overall toxic environment. After I saw what life was going to be like in this unit, I questioned why I signed up for six years of this. I did manage to find five guys in my platoon who were worth hanging out with. These were the only people I could depend on, as they weren't into drugs and they kind of resembled the type of friends I had in high school. One of these guys really stuck out. He was from Apple Valley, California and was a couple of years older than me. He had already been on a deployment to Iraq with the 25th Infantry Division and was pretty much a badass. This guy broke me out of my little Central Wisconsin bubble and taught me a lot about the world. He introduced me to a ton of great music and bands that I never heard of, got me super drunk for the first time in my life, and took me out for burritos the next day to cure my first hangover. These are the kind of fun things you have to do before your deployment to sort of ease the mood. We also went to a strip club for my first time ever. It was definitely not my scene, but I did order one of the best grilled cheese sandwiches ever. This guy was the kind of person you could depend on for anything. He would go out of his way to do anything to help you out. There were a few other people I liked, but this guy was by far my best friend during my time in and I am glad he was there.

I was only at my unit about a month and a half before we deployed to Iraq, which was about one year after I graduated high school, so I was nineteen and one of the youngest guys in the platoon. I was a little nervous to deploy because I didn't know what to expect. I was, however, finally getting to do what I signed up for.

We arrived in Kirkuk at night. When I stepped off of the plane, I was greeted with one of the worst smells ever. The smell is hard to describe, but it definitely came from the large amounts of trash, sewage, and random rotting things in the streets of that place, which was surrounded by burning oil fields that filled the air with black smoke plumes. All of the first timers, including myself, were wondering what the hell that smell was. The people who had been to that area before just laughed and said, "It's Iraq."

As soon as we got settled into our units on the main base, we went to sleep. A couple of hours later, "incoming" sirens woke me up, and there were a couple of distant explosions. I was pretty scared and asked my roommate (who had deployed once already) what to do, and he said I should "just go back to sleep." After a day of those sirens going off, they were no longer scary, and during my whole time there, the base got mortared about five times a day, sometimes a lot more. Sometimes we would go a couple days with none, but after the first day it was more of an annoyance than anything else. After a week of being there, the unit we replaced left, and we took over doing their missions.

I was one of four gunners in our platoon and I was in the turret of our vehicle whenever we were mobile. We would basically go on daily patrols, man checkpoints, and hunt down improvised rocket launchers when the main base was mortared. Additionally, we served as a quick reaction force from time to time. We were also "training" the Iraqi police force, but it seemed more like babysitting than training to me. Action on our deployment was sparse, other than fire we took from the enemy mortars.

It is really difficult to put into words what this place was like. During the summer, it got to 145 degrees, and in the winter, there were a lot of rain showers and a couple weeks of frost. Usually the sky was clear with no clouds in sight, but occasionally there were days when the air around us was either a hazy deep purple, a vibrant hazy orange glow, or just a flat out dust storm. I will never forget this night when we were on patrol and as we were coming over this hill, the night sky was lit up this creepy glowing orange color. As we crested the hill, I noticed the color came from one of the numerous burning oil fields that surrounded Kirkuk. This one night really sticks out in my mind because I made a conscious effort to stop and look at the color and everything it illuminated. In the flickering orange spectacle, I could see my whole body, my friend's face, my dickhead sergeant's mustache, the alley behind us, and the ramshackle little markets that were busy before the sun went down. The fire was so far away, but it was so big that I could feel the heat of it on my face. I don't know why, but this is my favorite memory of Iraq. It was the most surreal moment of my life.

The city was a disgusting landfill that closely resembled the massive burn pit located on the main base. I could tell the number one method for disposing of trash there was to throw it out in the streets and then brush it into any little space it would fit. The power lines hung into the streets like giant cobwebs and occasionally hooked on our vehicles when we were mobile, creating an electric light-show. There were canals of human excrement and urine. Sometimes on patrol, we had to walk through those rivers of shit. We also sweat like crazy and often had to wear diesel-soaked uniforms. I'm actually surprised that I did not get sick sooner than I did.

Toward the end of our deployment, seven of us came down with a severe illness while we were on patrol. The symptoms varied from man to man. For me, my vision became instantly blurry, and my ears started ringing. Soon my heart began to race, and I found that I could barely stand. I was dizzy, struggling to breathe, and I eventually developed a horrible migraine. Then I lost my sense of smell and taste. Initially I thought I just had some sort of influenza or something, but then I started rapidly losing weight. Over the course of two months, I went from about 220 pounds to 135 pounds, which I haven't weighed since I was in elementary school. I looked like one of the starving, disease-infested feral dogs that roamed the Iraqi wasteland in packs.

The situation was not handled well by my leadership. The seven of us were accused of malingering to get out of our duties. This really pissed me off, because my background demonstrated nothing but hard work and determination, not to mention the fact that there was no mistaking I was sick. To prove that there really was something the matter with me, I began getting the medical results to back me up.

I couldn't believe how badly I was being treated. I always did what I was told, I knew everything about my job, I always shot a perfect forty out of forty when we went to the range, and I never had a negative counseling statement. I wasn't involved in any trouble, and I was basically as good of a soldier as I could be. I finally got the help I needed after I developed a rash over my entire body. I also began suffering from severe pulmonary issues, and one of the other guys was developing lesions on his brain. We were sent out of Iraq.

When I arrived back in the United States, I was flown to Brooke Army Medical Center and was instantly isolated in a room where I couldn't be touched with bare hands. The staff there weren't sure what I had, if it was contagious, or how it might spread, so they also took airborne precautions. My nervous system was so messed up that my body could not even regulate my blood pressure. I couldn't even stand up without passing out, so I stayed in bed whenever I could and used a wheelchair for everything else. For a month I was basically a human experiment for the Army. I had so many needle sticks and tests being done that I did not know what the hell was going on. At one point, I was given some kind of medication that did nothing but give me seizures. Anything I tried to eat was not digested properly and was either vomited up or expelled as diarrhea. I was continually told by the medical personnel that they did not know what was wrong with me. I knew they were full of shit; they saw this stuff all the time and had been seeing it since the First Gulf War. I learned that my assumptions were correct, because I had an awesome nurse who told me they were lying to protect themselves and that there were numerous other soldiers with the same symptoms I was having. She told me to demand some sort of diagnosis as a way to protect myself. I am extremely thankful for that woman, because without her, I don't think things would have gone the way they did for me.

As time went on, I slowly began to regain my ability to walk, but I was still getting super dizzy and passing out every day. I tried anything I could to get my weight and strength back. Eventually, the Army decided to medically discharge me. They sent me back to my unit, which had now returned from Iraq, to wait until it was time for me to go. A couple of people I knew said I looked scary, like a sickly skeleton. The situation got really old very quickly. The worst part was when some asshole who had no idea what I was going through started getting on my case for being "lazy."

For morning physical training, I would try to walk as far as I could without passing out, having to sit down every couple minutes and let my heart rate catch up. My resting heart rate was always 140 to 170 beats per minute (bpm), which is partially in the anaerobic zone for a person with a normal heart rate. When I sat down, my heart rate would register at between 120 and 140 bpm. By 10 a.m. every day, my body was already shot, and I would feel like I just ran a marathon. Plus, there were the migraines, which were unimaginably painful. Most days, I would end up spending the majority of the day in bed. The doctors I was seeing at this time did not even know what to do with me, so I would go to appointments to be continually monitored. That's all they could do; every form of treatment they tried either didn't work or worsened my condition.

It has now been almost four years since I initially got sick, and I still have symptoms from my illness. Luckily, I have been gradually improving over the months, but I still cannot taste or smell anything, and I still wake up throughout the night with bad sweats and joint pains. Regardless of my symptoms, I continue to push through each day and do my best to hide any problems I am having. I do not want to be seen as weak or different than anyone else.

About three months after being discharged, I started going to the weight room at Stratford High School with my brother. I took it slow and safe to get back in the rhythm of things again, and I began realizing my favorite thing to do was now going to be the most challenging thing I have ever done. From that point until now, I have gained back almost all the muscle weight I had lost. I am currently enrolled at University of Wisconsin-Stevens Point, majoring in Clinical Laboratory Science, which I became very interested in when I first got sick. In my first semester, I decided to join the track and field team and throw discus once again, since I built myself back up. This has been the best thing I have done for myself and has helped me in unimaginable ways to reintegrate as a normal civilian. Not only does it feel great to be a member of a team doing my favorite sport, but I also feel like I have overcome a lot to get where I am as I write this, and I am happier than ever, as my hard work has paid off.

My life is pretty simple now. I go to classes, lift weights, attend track and field practice, and work on homework. I have an amazing wife who has supported me through every bit of my military ordeal and has even pushed me around to appointments when I was stuck in that damn wheelchair at the hospital. I am still pretty bitter about my time in the Army. The day I was discharged, I threw all my uniforms, medals, awards and anything military-related in a dumpster on the base. All I kept were my airborne wings, my Army patrol cap (because it keeps the sun out of my eyes when I go fishing), and all of my medical records. A month after being home, I received a call from my unit that they had awards for me from Iraq, and I told them to shove them up their asses. That was my last contact with anyone in my unit. I do not think I will ever be a fan of the military again, and I am not particularly proud of my service.

While this has not been one of the mainstream topics we hear about when we discuss veteran issues, diseases have been affecting active military members and veterans since there have been wars. During the American Civil War, the chance of dying from a disease caused by a micro-organism was higher than the chance of dying in combat. The Spanish influenza pandemic of 1918 killed a great deal of soldiers during the First World War. Agent Orange is a well-known chemical that took the life of many and is still affecting veterans of Vietnam. Since the Gulf War, and continuing to the current conflicts in the Middle East, soldiers and veterans have been developing unexplained illnesses and symptoms known as Gulf War Syndrome. There is no doubt in my mind that this is what I have. There are far too many veterans from that area of operations who have either the exact same or very similar symptoms to mine. This has been a pretty controversial illness, and I cannot believe that anyone still denies its existence. Thankfully, somewhat recently, this ailment has gained some recognition, and I believe it will continue to do so until the cause is fully known and understood.

I wanted to write this because I needed to tell my story. No veteran has the same story; therefore, no mass assumptions should be made about them. Each veteran has their own problems, accomplishments, and views on life. I also wanted to bring awareness to those veterans who have died, or are still dealing with issues, as I am, from either a chemical or biological origin.

NOT ALL VETERANS ARE THE SAME

By Zach Trzinski

Everyone is a winner, and everyone gets a trophy. Everyone is equal and the same no matter the who, what, where, when, why, or how about them. This is how my generation was raised, and it seems like there's no end in sight to this way of thinking.

On one hand, this is a good thing: no more racism, sexism, and classism (in a perfect world). On the other hand, this way of thinking also takes away from people who have done more than others have, and it also takes away from the drive to make you, yourself, a better person. This way of thinking also takes away the pride in who you are and what you do, because it doesn't matter what you actually do if everyone else is the same and deserves the same.

I wish I could say that the U.S. Army doesn't think this way, but it does. I was in the 82nd Airborne Division as an 11B (an infantryman). In the 82nd, there was a distinction between the two kinds of jobs someone could have. There were infantry personnel, who were known as "grunts" and POGs (persons other than grunts) who did all other jobs. Very clean cut. We had this outlook on the different jobs because of how different the jobs really are. In the infantry, your job could involve getting shot at, shooting back, losing a limb, dying, or all of the above. Most everyone knew it and accepted it. That doesn't mean we were happy about it, of course, but we accepted that it could be part of our job.

One POG job worth mentioning is that of parachute rigger. These men and women packed the parachutes for those of us who had to jump out of planes. They also checked over the chutes and fixed any problems that were found. They would only pack twenty-five static line para-chutes a day, no matter if it took them two hours or twelve hours to do all twenty-five. Parachute riggers are almost never deployed, so it is a mostly stateside job. Another POG job I'll mention is the job of mechanic. These guys will most likely have been deployed at least once with their battalion. They spend most of their deployments at a larger base, only leaving the walls once in a blue moon to go to a smaller base for a day or two. On deployment they, as you probably guessed, fix military vehicles and keep things running. Like the parachute riggers, they are not outside the wire, "John Ramboing" around the country. The last POG job I'll mention is the job of combat medic. Instead of fixing vehicles, they fix people. They can be attached to platoons or to an entire company. They can also spend all their time in a hospital either in America, Germany, Afghanistan, or elsewhere. They can also be the ones who are on the helicopters that pick up the dead or wounded. These guys get deployed probably just as often as infantryman do. Every job is different and each has its ups and downs.

Does this mean that an infantryman and a mechanic are equal? How about a parachute rigger and a combat medic? All four jobs are in the U.S. Army, and all four jobs can be found in the 82nd Airborne Division. Even though all four signed on the dotted line to serve the United States of America, all four are in the same division, and all four are considered veterans once they leave the military, all four are not the same nor are they equal. Each veteran experienced different things and made different sacrifices, depending on their job. Labeling them all as sacred veterans or assuming they were all "in the shit" should not only be a slap in the face to the men and women who were actually "in the shit," but also a slap in the face to the veterans that were not.

This perception that the general population has regarding all military veterans makes it hard for somebody like a parachute rigger to feel good about that job and take pride in it. They feel as if they have to live up to this un-achievable expectation or standard that civilians have set for them. So what if they only packed chutes and never left Fort Bragg the entire time they were in? They packed chutes for people like me, who jumped out of planes and who did not become sad pandas when their chutes didn't open. I'm grateful that the parachute riggers who packed every chute that I used knew what they were doing. If they weren't good at their job, I might not be here to write this. That is what people should be thankful for—veterans doing their jobs well. This means that if the general population wants to get to know "veterans," they're going to have to find them, get to know them as individuals, and learn what they did in the military instead of labeling everyone as the same and equal thing.

"In World War II," writes veteran and author William Manchester, "16 million Americans entered the armed forces. Of these, fewer than a million saw action. Logistically, it took 19 men to back up one man in combat. All who wore uniforms are called veterans, but more than 90 percent of them are as uninformed about the killing zones as those on the home front." When average civilians think about World War II veterans, they probably think about *Saving Private Ryan* or *Band of Brothers*. If, however, we take the numbers Manchester presents, that means for the seven infantrymen featured in *Saving Private Ryan*, there were another 133 soldiers supporting the infantry's mission. Those soldiers weren't featured in the movie, so no one thinks of that. I know I didn't when I first saw the movie.

Now imagine what would happen if you saw *Saving Private Ryan* and then thanked one of those 133 veterans for doing what you saw the infantry do in the movie. You thanked him for the wrong thing, something he never did. You didn't actually thank him for what he accomplished during his service.

While I was in, I remember having no respect for anyone who wasn't in the infantry. I felt as if they were too scared to do my job, so they chickened out and picked a safer job, therefore making them unworthy of my respect. I felt as if they didn't do anything important and we, the infantry, had to do everything ourselves because all the POGs were too worried about stupid shit like power and water on deployment. Now, after being out for over a year, I can look back and see times in which if it were not for those men and women, my brothers in arms would have been a lot worse off.

I remember this one POG who let us raid the battalion food stock once a month so we could supplement our diets of MREs and water with somewhat real food called hamburgers and hotdogs. There was another, a communications guy, who taught me how to rewire the trucks so that the radios would work in them. Then he "requisitioned" the necessary equipment from the mechanics and his own supply so I had enough to do it myself. He knew that it would take too long for it to be cleared so they could do it. Those two guys bent over backwards to help us when we needed it, even when they didn't have to and could have sent us through the long and painful way of getting things done. They deserve not just your respect, but also mine.

I wouldn't even consider my deployment Hell. I was never in a large-scale battle with bombs going off everywhere. Most of my deployment actually involved pulling extreme amounts of guard duty. This duty consisted of sitting in a guard tower by myself for hours on end staring off into the shitty landscape of southern Afghanistan, waiting to get shot at so I could shoot back and break the monotony of nothing happening. Action makes the time go by faster. I also had a foot patrol every other day. On these patrols, I got to go out and gamble with my life by playing hopscotch with IEDs in the road while also getting shot at, because just hopscotching IEDs isn't hard enough. I also got to go on a mounted patrol every other night for at least three hours at a time. On these patrols, I got to be a gunner and stare out into nothing because all the Afghans were too busy sleeping, like I should have been. The price for peace of mind I guess. But don't worry; just because we were not getting shot at as frequently on these night drives doesn't mean that the IEDs were sleeping. Those things got less sleep then I did. Because of them, I never wore the gunner's harness that was supposed to hold me in the truck in case of a roll over. I liked the odds of surviving getting thrown out of the truck from a blast better than the odds of getting smashed by a sixteen-ton vehicle as it rolled on top of me. This all meant that my schedule was to go out on a foot patrol, come back, and probably go right to three or four hours of guard, have off for a couple hours to fix every damn radio because they were always broken, then go on our night drive, get off and realize that for the next twenty-four hours, I would continue to be on a one-shift-on-one-shift-off guard schedule of three-hour shifts. Then, all I did was repeat that sequence until the day they decided to send me back home.

But we didn't forget to spice things up with a town clearing. This involved my platoon spearheading an assault into a hostile town held by the Taliban. Most of these missions involved multiple moving pieces and two to three companies with all of their platoons—about 250 people total. This was where most of the larger firefights took place. On the morning of one assault we made, our new platoon leader lost his foot from an IED. When the rest of my brothers and I were getting shot at or losing feet, it was hard to take it seriously when our commanding officer would ask us to babysit a cook for the assault of the town so that the cook could get his CAB (Combat Action Badge). None of us wanted to deal with a POG who didn't know what to do with himself and had nothing to contribute to the battle and to others' safety. The cook now became a liability to the rest of the platoon and put us all in danger just for a stupid award.

"When did you sleep?" I get asked that all the time. Well, you know when I get off guard right after the night of driving around? That is when I got to sleep, unless it was light out. Without the saintly AC we have here in America, it is impossible to sleep when the sun is up, because once the sun rose it was at least 110 degrees out. I was never good at trying to sleep in that kind of heat. That meant little to no sleep every day while on deployment.

To contrast, my sister joined the Navy, where they promise you a mattress wherever you go (unconfirmed, but it seems like it). Her deployment, from what I could gather, consisted of fixing electronics on the boat and delivering movies to the Captain of the ship almost every evening. Being on watch meant she was on call for when anything important broke. She also got to travel the world while doing this. How does Barcelona, Spain or Greece or even Dubai sound? Great to me. A lot better than Afghanistan. She never carried a gun, never shot a rifle. She just qualified in a simulator, which meant she shot a toy gun at a computer screen a couple of times. She never had to wear body armor, and she had the opportunity to go to a chow hall that cooked hot food. Sure they got to shoot missiles and had to deal with rough seas and other stuff I don't know about, but I'm pretty sure they never had to wonder if they should carry their Ka-Bar knife with them because of the possibility of extreme close-quarters contact.

How could you thank my sister the same way you would thank me on Veterans Day? Try for a second to understand that even if she didn't have to carry a gun, she did help keep a boat operational, and that boat could shoot missiles and help protect a carrier that has fast movers (jets). That is the infantry's support. Believe me, I was always happy to see a fast mover or helicopter or even a missile take care of the bad guys for me. When that happened, it meant that I didn't have to kick down the door and risk being shot or having the house blow up around me. Because she did her job, and because the pilots did theirs, I am here today. I'm thankful for that. You should be, too. Without POGs, there would be fewer infantrymen coming home to their families.

WANTING TO GO BACK TO HELL

By Cody Makuski

This is a tough one for me to talk about. My time in the military gave me some of the best times of my life, but it also gave me some of the worst. Thinking about those days makes me feel so blessed to be sitting in my recliner right now writing this essay. At the same time, however, I wish I was still over there to get some payback on those worthless fucks for what happened on the Giro mission. What happened on that mission is a big reason I struggled after I got home. The fifteen-day mission was a straight shot into the Wild West and back. It was a good fight.

Up to that point in my deployment, I had seen little of what Afghanistan had to offer. The platoon I was in got hit two by IEDs, which freaked us out, but that was pretty much it. I was in Reaper Platoon, and we were based at Combat Outpost (COP) Ab Band in Ghazni Province. Before we got there, the U.S. military hadn't sent a single soldier to that part of the province. It was a little-explored area of the country and a Taliban stronghold. We were there to take care of that part.

We had another platoon at a COP called Giro. They were known as Outkast Platoon, and their COP was located about forty-five kilometers away from where we were. Ab Band didn't receive much hassle from the Taliban, but Giro must have been their spot because our brothers over there were getting messed with all the time. Our brothers in Outkast Platoon were getting into sporadic firefights every time they went outside the wire. Eventually, because they were pinned down, the guys at Giro were running out of supplies. Our mission was to conduct a mounted convoy to COP Giro and bring them the supplies they needed.

Our plan was to leave in the middle of night, when the Taliban would hopefully be less active, and make it there by morning. I was scared shitless, if I'm being honest. I had already been blown up once. Add to that the fact that we were going on a forty-five-kilometer trek and I was lead truck. On top of it all, we would be traveling down HWY 1, the one and only paved highway in Afghanistan—an IED paradise. I got mentally prepared quickly, mainly by smoking a lot of cigarettes and thinking about my family back home. I hoped for the best, put my big boy pants on, and got ready for work. It was time to go.

Twenty or so armored trucks took off in the middle of the night on the mission. We kept a steady pace down HWY 1. We stopped at every previous blast sight to make sure the Taliban hadn't put any IEDs in the road before we left. We didn't have any problems making it to the outskirts of Giro. In fact, up to that point in the mission, everything was great. We had rigged up speakers in the truck so we could play our music while on the road. It seemed like we were going to make it there just fine. Then I saw the valley.

The only way we were getting to Giro was through that damn valley. We had soldiers walking in front of our trucks because we knew this was a great-looking chokepoint for the Taliban if they wanted to pick a fight. As the men in front scanned the ground for bombs, I remembered sitting in the driver's seat, thinking to myself that if something was going to happen, it would happen soon. We made it through the valley, and I drove off the road. About two minutes later, I heard, "BOOM!" I thought to myself, "What the fuck, didn't they follow me?"

About five trucks back, one of them had hit an IED pressure plate in the road. They didn't get off in time. Everyone was fine, though the truck was destroyed. We stopped our truck to overwatch a village straight in front of us. Strange things were happening in the village. The women and children were moving to one corner of the village, and the men were running from door to door. I knew we were probably fixing to get into a gunfight.

Taliban chatter started to come over the radio saying that they had eyes on us and that they were getting into battle positions. We didn't have time to sit and wait for the assholes to fight us, so after they got the blown-up truck loaded up on the wrecker, trucks started moving around the village and traveling toward our destination. We stayed up top on the ridge to provide overwatch just in case the Taliban decided to get into it with us. The route clearance patrol went first and then it happened again. Another "BOOM!" The second route clearance truck got blown up really badly by a huge IED. I figured they weren't alright just by seeing it.

We drove down toward them, and the Taliban fired a few rocket-propelled grenades (RPGs) in our convoy's direction. We couldn't see anyone, so we couldn't return fire. We figured they were somewhere tucked inside the village. My platoon sergeant called in a medevac, and they got the wounded guys out of there. Their Giro infill was over; mine was just beginning.

It took forever to get those blown-up trucks loaded up. It started to get really late in the day, and then it was dark. We surrounded the village with our big gun trucks and dared the Taliban to fuck with us again. They didn't. Then we got the call from our commander to continue mission. Our job now was to pull ahead of the pack and provide overwatch for the mechanic trucks, wreckers pulling blown-up trucks, and the trucks carrying supplies. We watched over for them as they continued to creep slowly around the mountain in front of us. Then it happened again. Two simultaneous explosions.

My heart just sunk at what I saw. One of the wreckers hit another IED pressure plate, and the explosion blew the cab off the truck and flung its occupants about one hundred meters. I figured they were dead. The truck behind them got hit pretty badly by the other huge IED. I was told to stay in my truck and not get out. Other soldiers rushed to their side and assisted the wounded. Believe it or not, everyone survived those two attacks.

I was upset, and I was scared, but most of all I was angry. We needed to get moving. We ran out of wreckers, so we called up to Giro to get some help pulling the blown-up trucks out. They spun up a quick reaction force (QRF) at Giro and sent them out to help. Then I heard another "BOOM!" in the distance. They just got hit by an IED as well.

The QRF now had its own shit going on, which meant we were now on our own. We stayed out there until the sun came up. When we finally made it to Giro, we were welcomed by our brothers from Outkast. They knew we just went through a little shit. Most of them just said, "Welcome to Giro," and we all laughed. Two days into the mission and we had already lost four trucks and had a handful of wounded men. We got some rest and prepared our trucks for another day. We knew what to expect now. We had the advantage. And that was the last time the Taliban got the last laugh.

"INCOMING!" I was working on my truck when a mortar landed on the other side of the COP's wall. Dirt and dust flew up in the air, and I knew I was lucky to be on the right side of things. I ran to the bunker and waited it out as several mortars came rocketing in from the sky. The Taliban knew we were there now, and they decided to mortar us every so often.

Now that we were at Giro, the higher-ups decided it was a good idea for us to run a few missions with Outkast. They wanted us to clear a village they previously couldn't because they lacked men. We went out on our first mission with them the next day. Instead of taking the roads, we took a more direct route to the village. We surrounded it with our guns and waited. Then we heard a thundering explosion.

After the mission, we traveled back to Giro and got mortared some more. It seemed like no matter what, the Taliban just wouldn't stop fucking with us. We spent the next three days at Giro helping them out as needed and downloading the supplies we brought them. Then it was time to head back to Ab Band.

Three days later, we were off—back to Ab Band. The difference in this trip was that we knew what we had coming for us. We were ready. The Taliban's fucking with us was going to end. We left in the middle of the day this time. We figured it didn't matter. We were pissed off, angry, and wanted to get back to our home base. Everything went fine for the most part in the beginning. Then we got to Route Rattlesnake.

Route Rattlesnake is a dirt road around fifteen kilometers long that was going to take us out to HWY 1 again. We knew it was probably loaded with IEDs. We were careful this time, scanning the roads vigilantly, stopping for any suspicious looking areas. It didn't take us long to find the first IED they buried. We were waiting on a controlled detonation when I started to hear sporadic machine gun fire coming from a tree line about 500 meters in front of us. This was it—I knew that this was going to be our payback to the Taliban.

I got out of my truck, got some cover, and began to return fire with my 240 machine gun. I gave them every round of ammunition I had on me. I sprayed that fucking tree line down so fucking hot that I don't know if I could have done a better job. My brother Meyer on the .50 caliber up top of the truck gave those assholes everything he had as well. We blew up the IED in front of us and continued on.

For the rest of the time out there we took some sniper fire, but that was it. I remember one time when I was putting fuel in my truck, and that sneaky sniper cracked one what seemed straight past my head. The crack of a bullet going past the side of your face is something you can never forget. It's a very distinct sound that I can still remember and hear in my head at times.

We made it off Route Rattlesnake without taking any casualties or losing any more trucks to bombs. It took about a week to go fifteen kilometers, but we made it back on HWY 1. We were pretty much home free. We made it to a big forward operating base called Sharana, and I remember how happy everyone was. It was so glorious to eat some real food and take a nice warm shower. I even found time to call home and talk to my family. I told them everything was fine and that I loved them very much. It was one of those bittersweet moments, knowing we had been to hell and back. It's absolutely amazing to me how people back home can go on with their daily lives while stuff like that is going on over there.

It seemed like the rest of deployment was a piece of cake after that hellacious fun. I'm not sure I ever smoked so many cigarettes in my life as I did on the Giro mission. It was a stressful time. It was the mission where the Taliban basically threw everything they had at us, and yet we still won the battle and made it home.

This is a story I really don't like talking about. It's this mission that basically defined Reaper Platoon 3-73 CAV's deployment to Ghazni. As valorous as it may be to the 82nd Airborne, I don't remember it that way. Brave men were wounded on this journey, some critically. There's no valor in the mission for me. If anything, only those who were wounded are valorous, because they alone felt the full effects of war. They suffered the pain. I just did my job and helped them as much as I could.

I've been out of the Army now for about a year, and I have been wondering for the longest time why I decided to get out. I miss my war and the crazy times I had over there. Now that I am home free, all I want is to go back. Being at war was one of the most unforgettable experiences of my life. I am who I am today because of those experiences.

Spending seven months in Afghanistan seemed like an eternity, though now I realize that it mostly came and went. Before I deployed, I remember thinking that the only thing I wanted to do was go overseas, get in the fight, and stick it to the bad guys; however, about three months in, the only thing I could think about was getting the hell out of there alive.

Every combat soldier dreams of going to war before they actually get the opportunity—that is what they sign up for. Luckily, I was of the chosen ones to proudly stand tall and serve my country during Operation Enduring Freedom.

About half way through the deployment, I wanted nothing more than to be at home, safe and sound in my barracks room with a case of beer and a relaxing song on the stereo. Then I got blown up. That's a whole other story. Suffice it to say, though, that my life flashed before my eyes, and I knew that I had just defeated death. It was then that I finally became worry-free. That was my mindset during our trip to Giro. And after we made it back from there, I breezed through the rest of the deployment. I embraced the suck, continued our combat missions, got into some good gunfights, and then came home.

But when I got home, I really wasn't "home."

Home to me at that point in time was a tent in the middle of a desert. Home to me wasn't the alarm clock going off in the morning, waking me up to go to work; instead, it was the incoming sound of a mortar round in the middle of the night—that's how I knew it was time for work. Home back in the states just isn't the same. I still feel lost.

I'm willing to bet that most soldiers who deploy in combat operations, if they're being really honest with themselves, do feel that sudden urge to go back and continue the good fight once they've returned stateside. It's something I never quite understood until I heard a presentation about it in my veteran reintegration class at the University of Wisconsin-Stevens Point. I found it funny when they said most soldiers are adrenaline junkies who cannot stop looking for that sudden rush. I thought to myself, "That's not me." The more and more I thought about it, though, I realized it was. All those good jumps out of airplanes and all those thrilling missions in the desert must have gotten me hooked. I was one of those people. It was the most exciting thing I've ever done in my life, and I loved every minute of it.

I think a lot of soldiers have a hard time when they get out of the service and miss being at war because they have finally come to the conclusion that they will never be that "cool" again. It sounds funny, but it really is true. When soldiers get out or the service, they have a hard time finding that one job or activity that can substitute for their addiction to the danger of war.

Every soldier misses his time in the service one way or another. It's just a part of who we are. If any veteran came to me and said they are so glad to be out and don't miss a thing about war, I would call a bluff on his part instantly. I think that's why I found the presentation on combat addiction interesting—because you don't even know it's a real thing until people are actually talking about it. It was very interesting to hear about how the brain triggers you to want to be back in Afghanistan and fighting alongside your brothers.

I believe combat addiction is a semi-curable disease after you've come to the conclusion that you will never be that "Cool Guy" in Afghanistan fighting bad guys again. We can all move on from the past in one way or another, but the thoughts of the good and bad times of war will always be in our heads, and there will always be that one little thought of "I wish I was back" rattling in our brains. I just pray that this will only be in my time, so my daughter can live in peace and freedom for the rest of her life. Like I said, those were some of the greatest and worst times in my life, stories that will be with me for the rest of my time on earth.

EARNING A SEAT AT THE TABLE

By Sara Poquette

I joined the military as a young, naive eighteen-year-old. At the time, I was unaware that I would spend more than a decade fighting to prove my worth as a soldier, a female, and eventually, a veteran.

My deployment to Iraq in 2004 as a broadcast journalist with the Wisconsin Army National Guard was my first experience with the "female soldier" stereotype.

While I was in Iraq, my job was to produce video news packages about service members and coalition forces working together to rebuild Iraq's infrastructure. This meant I would embed with other soldiers in the field to capture the story of the work they were doing. The goal was to allow friends, family members, and the American public a unique perspective on the work that their sons, daughters, husbands, and wives were performing every day.

When I worked with a group of soldiers for the first time, my presence was often met with an eye roll, complete dismissal, or a lame attempt to flirt. I would watch as some would immediately stop a conversation or task and make a beeline for anywhere other than within 150 feet of me. I would overhear grunts of frustration or the tail end of a sexually explicit comment. It was easy for me to see and feel that I was viewed as a burden, not an equal. It was often assumed I would need special accommodations for sleeping and showering when in fact I would eat, sleep, shower, and shit in the same place as my male counterparts—exactly as I had been trained to do.

On November 3, 2004, twenty-one mortars landed inside the forward operating base where I was stationed. One of those rounds destroyed the shower trailer I had been in not ten minutes before the attack started. Later that day, a vehicle in my convoy was hit with a vehicle-born improvised explosive device. I remember seeing the explosion, feeling the pressure wave, and driving through the biggest fireball I had ever seen. After we had reached safety, one of the male soldiers told me that I was the only female on the convoy and that this was the first time his unit had been under attack.

He told me I was "bad juju."

At this point, I had been so used to the comments that I laughed out loud. On the inside, I was shocked he would say such a thing to me. I realized in a therapy session seven years later that this was a defining moment of my perpetual self-defeat.

I came home from that deployment a few months later only to be met with another gender stereotype. I was initially comforted by the fact that I was seeing a female health-care provider and assumed I could be candid—and that she would understand where I was coming from.

I was wrong.

As I sat at the VA hospital for the very first time, I was explaining to the nurse some of the things I was experiencing—hypervigilance, panic attacks, and emotional numbness to name a few—and I asked her if it was possible that I was experiencing post-traumatic stress disorder (PTSD). She made no eye contact with me and responded with a laugh, stating, "There is no way you could have PTSD, because PTSD is only seen in men who saw combat."

The fact is, I did see combat.

Did she say that I hadn't because I was female? What about the mortars that landed near me on a weekly basis? Is that not enough? What about the IED? These are some of the questions I asked myself on a continual basis, as I doubted my service and my worth as a female soldier.

Unfortunately, I still ask myself these questions. This causes me to hesitate in sharing my experiences, as if

I'm protecting myself from yet another blow to my self-esteem. I never know how my stories will be received.

I'm working hard to change that, but it's difficult as I continue to run into those that don't understand the ramifications of their ignorance.

Recently, ten years after my deployment, I met a fellow veteran who had deployed to Iraq, and we began talking about our time overseas. I was happily engaged in the conversation until he asked me if I had ever fired my weapon while I was deployed.

I knew where he was going with this.

I knew he wanted to play to the stereotype that females were behind the lines and never in danger. I knew he wanted a good laugh from his fellow veteran buddies about the girl who didn't fire her weapon but dared to say she was a combat veteran.

I said no.

He looked at me and said, "Well, I guess you could still have a seat at the table with the other veterans."

I regret not asking him if my Combat Action Badge paid for that seat.

After all the bullshit I've gone through, I'm honestly quite shocked when I share my stories and they're embraced and met with genuine support, especially from my male veteran peers. I'm fortunate to have married a veteran who tells me—and everyone else we meet—how great my story is. And yet, I still spend so much time feeling the pain of not being taken seriously.

I know that I shouldn't, and that those individuals and the institution that fed that stereotype shouldn't have that kind of effect on me after all these years, but knowing something and doing something are sometimes very different things.

I earned my Combat Action Badge, and I've earned my seat at the table. I don't want special treatment or a national female soldier day. I want everyone—both civilian and veteran alike—to know that there are thousands of female soldiers who served as I did, and their service is just as important and impactful as the male soldiers they stood shoulder to shoulder with.

FINISHING FIFTY

By Brett Foley

People would ask me, "Why are you running fifty miles? That's crazy!" I would usually just smile at them and say, "Yeah, but it's for a good cause. We're running to raise money for The Mission Continues, an amazing nonprofit that helps veterans transition home." After months and months of this, it became a kind of learned response without any emotional attachment to what I was saying. But it wasn't until about two months before the race date when I actually thought, "Holy shit, I'm actually gonna have to do this."

It was at that point that I started to worry. I had been training, but I was nowhere near where I wanted to be. I had been running eight to thirteen miles every other day, but I hadn't even run a marathon distance. I had a hard time fitting in the training between work, school, the police academy, and things around the house. I was worried that when race day came around, I would get to about twenty miles and my body would just shut down because it had never gone that far before.

Eventually, I just adopted the mentality of "whatever happens, I'm gonna run until I pass out or something breaks." I felt that I could live with that, as long as I gave the race everything I had and didn't quit just for the sake of quitting. I also thought about all the people who have supported me and all the people counting on me to do this, and I knew that I couldn't let them down.

Things didn't really kick in until I picked up my race packet that cold and rainy October evening with my racing partner, Dave. It was there that I had somewhat of an "oh shit" moment. I started to panic a bit and started thinking of all of the stuff I was going to need for the race. It felt a lot like the times I was getting ready for a deployment or a couple weeks in the field—the night before, I would run through everything that I needed and shove it all into a bag.

Dave and I went to bed around 10:00 p.m. The nervousness started to kick in again, and I tossed and turned most of the night. After a solid hour or so of sleep we got up and started getting all of our stuff together for the race. I packed all of the things I thought I would need, and my mom and dad showed up to give us a ride to the start, which was over fifty miles away.

As we were driving up the Door Peninsula of Wisconsin, I remember thinking that it was a long fucking drive—that it was going to be a hell of a time to run this distance back. It was raining and really windy, which only added to my nerves. Once we got to the starting line, I felt like when I use to get on the plane for a deployment, and all of the nervousness and uncertainty rushed over me as we waited for the race to start.

The national anthem played as the wind whipped a tattered American flag next to the starting line. Eventually, the announcer initiated the start of the race, and I started to trot along with the rest of the people who had nothing better to do that day than run fifty miles in the cold.

It gave me some comfort to see that the big group of people was moving about the same pace that Dave and I were. A lot of people started out walking the hills to conserve energy, and we all trotted through the first five miles or so with ease. I looked around and noticed all the smiles on people's faces and wondered, "What are those faces going to look like at mile thirty-seven?"

When we made it to the first checkpoint, we picked up some supplies we thought we were going to need. We shed or put on clothes depending on how hot or cold we were. I grabbed a CamelBak that I had filled with electrolytes. I was worried because I succumbed to heat exhaustion several times while I was in the Marines, but I knew that I would be alright if I stayed hydrated and went overboard on the electrolytes.

My compression shorts had already started to chafe a bit, so I grabbed some nut butter from my supplies and applied a generous amount to my undercarriage. We then took off running again. The next couple miles were actually pretty pleasant. Dave and I talked most of the time. We talked politics, past experiences, race issues, and other things. We ran through several small villages and through a couple of different checkpoints.

I think it was about mile fifteen when I started thinking, "Yep, I've had enough. This can stop anytime." But I knew that there were still thirty-five miles to go. Dave and I agreed to slow down to a trot. We continued to take our two-minute walk breaks in between running for about ten minutes. I told Dave, "I think as long as we stick to the game plan, we'll make it." In my head I thought, "You are full of shit. Your ankle hurts and you've never run this far in your life."

Dave and I kept trudging along, trying to make conversation as we went. The relay team runners were starting to fly past us at a pretty consistent rate, which I thought would be really discouraging. It wasn't. They all had something nice to say as they went past. Thing like, "Go Solo!" or, "You guys are crazy." I think one lady called us rock stars. It was nice to have that little extra bump of confidence. That continued for the entire race, and I thank all of those people who had something positive to say as they ran past, because that really pulls you out of the darkness in your head.

Dave and I came into the twenty-five-mile mark and stopped at the aid station. Our wives, Whitney and Ashley, and my parents loaded us up with some supplies, gave us some words of encouragement, and we set out again. We pushed on and went up and down some huge hills on the course. My ankle really started to hurt, and I could feel it swelling in my shoe. Every time we stopped, I tried to stretch it out, but that would only help for about five minutes or so.

I began to think that thirty miles was going to be a really big milestone for us and that we only needed to get to that point. My head started to take over at this point and tell me things like, "Yeah, you'll probably make it to thirty miles, but there's no way you are gonna do another twenty after that." Dave saved me here, because he kept talking to me, and it took my mind off of the pain and the negative thoughts I was having.

We had humped our asses up a huge hill when I noticed an American flag wrapped around a driveway marker because the pole had fallen. I went over and unwrapped it from the marker and repositioned it on the holder. Then I walked back over to where Dave was waiting for me. "Yep, that makes me feel better," I told him. It was then that I realized that there were a lot of awesome things and great people around me, and that I just needed to look for inspiration to keep my mind in a positive place. That picked me up for miles and somewhat masked the pain I was feeling below my waist.

We kept running and running, and eventually both Dave and I talked less and less. I think we were both battling demons in our minds telling us this wasn't possible and that we should stop. I eventually entered full blown zombie mode and just started staring at the ground. It felt a lot like the times when we used to go on long marches with heavy-ass packs strapped to our backs. After a while your mind just shuts off and you go on autopilot. Some guys even fall asleep while they're walking. I didn't want to talk; I just kept thinking about how bad my ankle hurt and how much my hips were starting to hurt. It was about this time that my wife, Whitney, hopped in to run a leg with us. I enjoyed the company, but I wasn't really in the talking mood anymore. She and Dave started talking about things, and I listened in on the conversations to take my mind off the pain.

We got to the next checkpoint and loaded up on supplies again. I remember my dad saying something like, "Keep going—you guys are gonna make it." I think that and a banana picked me up a bit and snapped me back to reality. Dave and I stretched and got ready to head out again. My mom jumped in with us this time, and we scooted through a really hilly portion of the course. She and Dave talked, and I again listened to the conversation to distract myself. I began to feel that I was running low on energy. I think my mom noticed this and tried to give me some words of encouragement.

After we got to the next checkpoint, we stopped and I stretched again. My groin muscles were really starting to hurt now. Dave and I started back out. We said to each other that we only needed to make it to the 40 mile mark and that would be a huge milestone for both of us. But in the meantime, I was really starting to fall deep into the darkness of my head, and I began to be enveloped in a lot of negative thoughts. It was right around then that I remembered a time that Dave had said he enjoyed telling the voice in his head to shut up when he felt like he couldn't go any further. I decided to give that a shot. I told myself to stop thinking negatively and just run the damn race.

We kept going until we got to the next checkpoint. Dave's wife, Ashley, hopped in with us and we took off again. I remember thinking, "Ashley is four months pregnant, and if she's out here running, you can at least go for a little while longer." So we kept on moving. It wasn't long before I started to get angry from the pain. That was, until I saw a man pushing a wheelchair in a Ghostbusters costume. He was pushing a young man with some cognitive disabilities through the race in a full-blown Ghostbusters suit. I thought that that was amazing, and I started to think about all of the good people that I had met through the whole ordeal. I started thinking that there were so many good people in my life, and that I should quit complaining because they were counting on me to make it through this.

Mile forty brought on all the clichés: I was out of gas, I'd burned my matches, the bell had tolled, and the fat lady had sung. I was really struggling at that point. Dave and I were really fighting for every mile marker we came to. We were trying to stay positive, and I was really impressed with both of us for sticking it out for forty miles. A year before the race, if Dave would have told me that we were going to go for a forty-mile run, I would have laughed at him and told him I was going back to bed.

We pushed on, with Dave's cousin, Damien, tagging along with us, offering words of encouragement and trying to keep our minds off of the pain and monotony of running. I started to get really frustrated and began picking up the pace. I thought, "Well, I'm either gonna break or finish this thing." Dave, Damien, and I pushed on and tried to make it to the next checkpoint. My legs and ankle were on fire, and I just wanted everything to be done. I pulled into the last checkpoint a little ahead of Dave and Damien. I saw Whitney there, and she greeted me as I pulled in. I stuffed my mouth with an apple.

I was beaten, and I just wanted to sit down and stop. I had had enough twenty miles earlier, and now things were horrible. Whitney hugged me and said, "Remember what you're doing this for." That was when everything just snapped inside my head. All the darkness went away, and I thought, "She's right. There are guys that would kill to be able to use their legs again or take another step, or hug their children, or hold their wives. Some of them will never be able to do that again, so what the fuck do you have to complain about? Yeah, your legs are hurting a bit. Get over it, and suck it the fuck up." I gave her a kiss and took off.

I felt like I had a clear head again, and I thought, "You are going to finish this race if it kills you." I thought about all the people I had deployed with and all the good times that I had. I thought about all the messages on Facebook from people telling us what a great cause we were supporting, and I thought about my family and how they have always been there to support me. I sure as hell wasn't going to let any of them down.

What happened next I can't really describe, but all the pain just went away. My legs, my hips, my ankle—all the pain just stopped. So I took off. I ran from mile marker to mile marker. I threw some Taproot on my MP3 player and just enjoyed the run. I couldn't believe what was happening and how good I felt. I thought, "Holy shit, I'm really gonna make it. There's only four miles left." Then my mom and dad pulled up with the van. I yelled to them and asked them what time it was. They said I had twenty minutes to the cutoff. I told myself, "You can cover a couple miles in twenty minutes, no problem." So I picked up the pace.

I got to mile forty-nine, and my mom got out of the van to run with me. I was cruising and exhilarated that I was actually going to finish this thing. I blew into the finish line with a couple minutes to spare. I remember thinking, "this is awesome," and that I didn't remember too many times in my life when I felt like that. I was proud of myself for doing it and honored that I got to share the experience with such great people.

Whitney kept telling me to go put on some warm clothes because I was soaking wet and it was freezing outside. I told her that I had to stay to watch Dave come across. Several minutes later, Dave and Ashley came running up to the finish area. Dave crossed, and I could see the sense of accomplishment wash over him. We had struggled together for eleven hours, and now we could rest. It's hard to describe what an amazing feeling it is to suffer with someone and come out victorious. It's something I missed after I left the military. As he came across the line, I hugged him, and we just took in the feelings of the moment, the accomplishment, the love from family, the pain, the joy, everything. We could feel our friends and family staring at us. I'm sure they felt it, too. It was a perfect moment. You only get a couple of those in your life, so cherish them when they come.

Overall, the race was one of the best things I've ever done in my life. I learned a lot about myself, and I learned a lot from Dave. I am truly blessed to have such amazing people in my life to help me get through the things that I have struggled with. I don't think I would've made it here without the support from my friends and family. I'm especially thankful for my wife, Whitney, for putting up with all of my bullshit when she didn't have to. The whole process helped me battle the demons I was dealing with after the military, and I think sharing my story has helped others as well.

WAR FOLLOWED ME HOME

By Zachary Ruesch

I am a veteran. I answered our nation's ongoing call for volunteers to serve in the military. I served seven years a soldier in the Wisconsin Army National Guard. I was a part-time soldier, a weekend warrior, a nasty girl. We were considered to be a "lesser" force. But for me, the National Guard was a perfect compromise. It allowed me not only to fulfill my sincere desire to deserve, in some way, my status as a spoiled, ignorant citizen of this nation, but also to remain close to my daughter.

LEAVING HOME

While serving, I recognized that it simply was not enough to wear the uniform part-time and perform my peaceful duties. I needed to deploy. When I looked in the mirror and lay in bed at night, I thought so very often of those who had gone before to fight in our nation's previous battles and who were currently deployed fighting today's. It felt incredibly wrong to have people thank me, shake my hand, and pay attention to me when I had done absolutely nothing to deserve it. Plus, a part of me wanted to be tested by the experience of violence in combat. As sick and twisted as this admission may be to some, it is the truth.

I deployed to Afghanistan in 2009 with the 951st Engineer Company, Sapper, from Rhinelander, Wisconsin as part of the 276th Engineer Battalion from Virginia. The battalion consisted of a company each from Virginia, California, Michigan, and Wisconsin. I volunteered to deploy alongside my brethren to serve, as I understood, a higher calling, to fulfill myself. Had I not done so, I would have judged myself, and on my last day upon this earth,

I knew that I would have regretted every breath I stole. I went to war wanting it.

Our mission in Afghanistan was route clearance. Simply put, we made roads passable for other units. We supported others by going before them and clearing the way. Most civilians who read this will think little about this statement. But for anyone who has ever driven or walked a road in a hostile land, you know.

What we encountered in clearing routes was a combination of difficult terrain and weather (at times), ambushes, and the ever-dreaded improvised explosive device (IED). The last of these was our purpose. We found and cleared them from our vehicles and on foot. This short paragraph, and the few words here, could be all I ever use to describe deployment. And probably for most civilians, it would be enough. They might inquire to know more, but in the end, it would be very difficult to paint a picture they want to see.

Each of us experienced something different over there. Even those of us who served together in the exact same place, at the exact same time, saw and felt something slightly different based on our understanding of this world and our lives. Still, what we experienced, no matter how differently we saw it, brought us together. What kept us alive was each other.

I could write about violence and how you become intensely aware of its presence. It consumes you, because every piece of equipment, knowledge, training, procedure, and thought is geared toward defeating the threat. On my first day in country, there was a suicide bombing in the city near our forward operating base (FOB). It was real. The first time you experience someone trying to kill you or your friends, you cannot help but be snapped into a new reality—something more real than reality, perhaps.

I remember the first explosion vividly. It is seared into my mind. And despite the fact my comrades were uninjured, the knowledge of it changed things. I saw the dirt, dust, flames, and smoke as an eighty-pound piece of tire floated through the air effortlessly and the dust settled to reveal the wreckage, carnage, and effects of war. It was real and concrete. What you see with your eyes, though, is only part of what war does and is.

I remember a silence washed over me as I sat there helpless to do anything other than keep watch and listen. As the deployment continued, we would see more violence, with human casualties—the victims of bureaucratic necessity intended to ensure the safety of the United States government, its people, and allies. Oh, and the spread of freedom and democracy. As I pushed through it all, I was consumed. It was in me, and so it remains.

As the deployment comes to us, we become the deployment. We accept the way it is, and it begins to feel like "normal life." Then, when we come home to our real, normal lives with family, children, friends, and the everyday plethora of people who say "thank you," we come to realize many do not appreciate or fully understand the sacrifice, right or wrong. Sometimes, this includes us.

COMING HOME

When I first returned, life at home was beautiful. I felt incredibly happy, motivated, driven, focused, and whatever other positive adjective you might conjure up to describe it. But there were little things that stuck with me and manifested themselves. For instance, being alone was incredibly difficult. I remember the experience of realizing I was completely alone for the first time in a very long time. I had never really noticed being alone, but in that moment, it was overwhelming. My chest felt heavy, and my heart was pounding. I tried to think of it as a positive thing, but I was tainted with fear, and then I thought about not having a weapon. I felt naked without one, especially when I would wake up in the middle of the night unsure of where exactly I was. Good thing the doors and windows were securely locked and I was in an elevated position, where I could better deter aggression. After my fiancé would leave for school or work, I would literally pace the apartment contemplating what I should do to keep busy and to be normal again. I thought about that a lot—how to be normal—but I was too anxious to do anything but pace.

After being home for a few weeks, I returned to work and school, and I ended the relationship with my fiancé, which had thrived during my deployment. This occurred within a matter of a week and half. I found myself in a difficult situation personally. I was consumed by confusion, anger, and sadness. I do not know how to put into words how profoundly "out of it" I was. And then shit got real.

I started dreaming of things I had experienced. I started imagining scenes of violence from my deployment, and they would mix with my daily life as a civilian. While driving for most people is almost mindless and instinctual, for me, it was labored. I was constantly reminded of possible signs of IEDs. The worst experience was turning left or turning right. As my focus shifted with the turn, intense fear of what threat approached from the opposite direction tore at my mind. As far as other drivers were concerned, I'm sure I looked and drove normally, but the whole time my mind would be racing, my heart beating fast, my palms sweaty with anxiety.

I remember one night, well after dark, I was walking down a hall at school and someone came running up behind me from around the corner. Without thinking, I whipped around to confront what my body assumed was a threat. My fists clenched, and I turned sharply and directly toward the threat, my eyes and face focused and ready, bristling with aggression. The kid stopped dead in his tracks with a look of horror upon his face. Our eyes locked, and he stumbled back a few steps, with his hands up in front, palms open and up attempting to place a barrier between himself and me, all while calling me off with pleas of peace. This moment occurred in a split second, but it felt like an eternity in my mind. Luckily, something snapped me back to reality, and I apologized sheepishly. I'll admit though, I felt simultaneously happy and ashamed. The rush was intense, and I had missed it.

Walking around campus was an intense experience, as the number of people and crisscrossing paths bothered me to no end. There was no control. And if another dude was not making way for me on a sidewalk and he dared make eye contact, he learned that shit wasn't going to fly. I also found myself sleeping in my sleeping bag (whenever it was that I was able to sleep) either in bed, on the floor, or on the couch. In fact, I slept on my brother's couch for nine months as I slowly put myself back together.

BECOMING ME AGAIN

It was most assuredly not easy to become me again. I give a great deal of credit to family, especially my brother, comrades from my unit, and comrades and friends I met through school. These people supported and encouraged me to push forward and do what I needed to be successful and heal. For me, it all came together through opportunities in college. It was there I not only learned a great deal about the world around us, but also about myself and my experiences.

School was a challenging experience, though. Attending classes on campus, taking notes, reading, taking more notes, writing, and studying were immensely difficult. To survive, I approached school as my mission. I made it my goal to be there early, do what I needed to do, and return home with only the most minimal tasks remaining. I did this because I wanted to "get lost" when I was home. I drank nearly every single night until the beer made me care, think, and feel less. This helped me to find sleep.

In class, I sat in a position where I might observe and more easily identify any possible threat, and to be sure, I contemplated and planned courses of action in order to counter any possible attacks that might occur. I also talked with most of the professors, especially if I was having a hard time. This was difficult to do, as I was resistant to the idea of appearing weak. But, I did it. And, it helped. They recognized me and helped me to improvise, adapt, and overcome.

I also became involved with the Veterans Club on campus. It was my Godsend. There, I met others who understood and knew what I had been through. It took time, but strong, trusting bonds grew. I found a place and people with whom I might express myself and be understood. They were like me.

In class and around campus, I felt surrounded by an unending supply of snot-nosed children who were more concerned about entertainment, television, sleeping in, how gorgeous they appeared, drinking, and enjoying life than they were about the violence being endured by their peers in their names in places half-the-world away—places many of them undoubtedly were unable to identify on a map.

Through the Veterans Club, I found a safe place to be, to express myself, and to develop friendships. I started to slowly recognize I was not alone in this world. I started noticing the haircuts, boots, backpacks, and t-shirts of those who were just like me. We would see each other and nod as we walked past one another on the way to class. In the classroom, we would instinctively migrate to the same table or corner of the room. We were drawn to one another because of our commonalities. Branch and rank mattered little. We were just veterans.

The university itself supported us by allowing a counselor with combat experience to support veteran needs on campus by lending us a space for sessions. I, and many others, found this asset to be incredibly invaluable at certain points in our adjustment processes. We were also lucky enough to receive the dedicated support of two tutors in our office. In addition, the chancellor and so many others made it a point to check in with us from time to time to hear how we were doing.

There are so many people I could list who have done much to advocate for and support veteran needs, sometimes directly and personally. For instance, an older gentleman somewhere in age between my father and grandfather who works as a custodian made it a point to say hello each morning as I sat reading or studying in the Veterans Club office. I remember many times our simple exchanges turned into thoughtful and open conversations. He sometimes just listened. I'm not sure he knows how much I appreciate what he did.

As things came together for me and my life improved, I continued to meet others who were returning home from the military. There were a few who had been in a combat zone literally only a handful of days previously. Their determination to return to school so soon after coming home was astounding. But then again, I already knew what they did not; it is not always easy to come to home. I have heard many veterans say that being deployed was so much easier than being home. This is sad to admit, but very true.

WE GREETED VIOLENCE WITH VIOLENCE

By Aaron Lewis

Angry, violent, and dangerous are some of the adjectives that are commonly used to describe veterans. I wish I could say they were wrong, but they're not—at least not completely. The Army has its own way of making soldiers angry, violent, and dangerous—at least when they need to be. Those who go on to serve in a combat role need these attributes to stay alive. I was a combat engineer in the Army, and without those attributes, I might not be here today. The truth is that every single man, woman, and child has these feelings in them from the moment they are born until the day they die. The only difference is that soldiers need to draw strength from them, and use them to survive. Civilians have the luxury of being fearful of them. Most will never have to feel what it's like to need them. When veterans come home from war, though, they may start to fear what they needed to survive. They may fear what all the anger, violence, and danger have done to them. I know I do.

"The wars on terrorism," writes Jessica Stern of the Harvard School of Public Health, "are exposing our military personnel to unprecedented levels of psychological injury. And yet, nearly a decade in, we remain unprepared to handle the growing numbers of personnel seeking treatment." This is the unfortunate reality. Some of the smartest doctors in the world can't seem to figure out exactly why soldiers suffer mental injuries, nor can they figure out how to fix them. Too bad that doesn't stop us from sending wave after wave of young men and women into battle with little more than a hope that they will be okay.

I don't know if the majority of our society is even aware of this true cost of war. It's been more than a decade since the wars in Iraq and Afghanistan started, and we still don't know how to help our heroes after they return from war. I know if I didn't know how to do my job after more than ten years, I sure as hell wouldn't still have one. That's another reasons some people fear veterans—they fear the unknown. There is no one answer when it comes to healing the mind. The right answer for me might send other veterans running for the hills, or worse, it could cause them to have a violent reaction if they don't agree with it.

My old platoon sergeant would always say, "We greet violence with violence." These words were my motto throughout my time in the service. My interpretation of this is that any time my life, my unit, or innocent civilians' lives were in immediate danger, I had to rise up above fear and become the darkness that was my fear. I did this by digging deep into my heart and using the emotions that I fear to instill fear into those who would do harm to me. I would become angrier than my enemy. I would use this anger as fuel for violence, and an angry, violent soldier is the most dangerous weapon in the U.S. military's arsenal.

As Rudyard Kipling pointed out, people sleep peacefully in their beds at night only because rough men stand ready to do violence on their behalf. I became that rough man, and I was ready to do violence on your behalf. All the men and women I served with were. Soldiers learn to become violent to protect the people they love. When we move from being a soldier to becoming a veteran, and we are forced to intermix with civilians, we don't just forget the things we have learned. Veterans bring that baggage with them.

If you were to ask me if veterans are angry, violent, and dangerous, the answer is yes. These are the traits that are publicized by the media. Vets do, however, bring more to the table than meets the eye. Leadership is one of the most sought after qualities. In the words of T.S. Eliot, "Only those who will risk going too far can possibly find out how far one can go." This is the type of thinking that a veteran leader is likely to use. We have a desire to win because to lose is to die. This invites creative thinking and unusual methods of observation that our civilian counterparts sometimes just can't understand. The military is a breeding ground for great people. I read somewhere once that "ordinary people think merely of spending time. Great people think of using it."

Before I joined the Army, I poured concrete: walls, floors, sidewalks, and driveways. I worked from sun up till sun down. I gave it my all. I worked till I had nothing left to give. After three years of backbreaking work, when all the dust had settled, I found myself out of a job. My life took an unexpected turn. I had never thought about the military before this point, but without other job prospects, I decided to go talk with a recruiter. When I was in school, a subject that had interested me was engineering. I told the recruiter what I wanted to do, and he recommended 21B Combat Engineer. That was it! I figured that if I joined the Army for a couple of years, and if I took advantage of the free education, I would come back and have the skills I needed to land a sweet job in a field I was interested in. Long story short: wrong, wrong, wrong!

I signed a contract for three years and sixteen weeks. I was sent to Fort Leonard Wood, Missouri for basic and advanced individual training (AIT). I quickly learned that I was not going to be trained to do the things engineers in the civilian world typically do. I embraced it for what it was, though, and I learned how to arm and disarm land-mines, make booby traps, set up C-4 charges, and a whole mess of other cool things. It was an exciting new chapter in my life, and I wasn't going to focus on the negative portion. I decided to embrace all the things that I might not have otherwise experienced if I wasn't there.

When I got to my first duty station, I found out what I was going to be doing for the next couple of years. It is called route clearance, and it was a new task that was created because of the type of guerilla warfare being fought in Iraq and Afghanistan. The enemy wasn't inflicting casualties with small arms fire, but rather with land mines and Improvised Explosive Devices (IED). I trained with my unit for two years on change detection and studied the enemy's tactics before our unit was called upon to deploy. In these two years, I set myself apart from my peers by performing exceptionally well at identifying minute details. This helped me not just as a specialty in my job, but with every aspect of my life. I can't remember how many times I was reminded that, "Success is achieved through sacrifice and attention to detail." By this measure, I was sure to be a success. With my keen eye and attention to detail, I was assigned to be the lead Husky driver in our patrol. Husky vehicles are used to detect IEDs, and they usually ride out in front of a route clearance patrol. While it is every person's job to be scanning for threats continuously, studying enemy activity, and recognizing common trigger points, the person on point in a patrol always has the greatest responsibility for this.

I was asked once exactly how many IEDs I had found in Iraq. I told the guy who asked me to go run past the targets on a live fire shooting range and report back to me exactly how many times he was fired at. I told him that he probably wouldn't remember the ones that missed by a mile, but he sure as hell would never forget the one that hit him. I can tell you about a handful of IEDs I encountered in vivid detail. The rest have either faded away in memory because I have tried to forget them, or they were just simple, mundane explosives. It might sound crazy to think of a deadly weapon as mundane, but when you see the same thing day after day, it loses that memorable quality.

I mentioned earlier that I trained for two years in change detection, but what does that mean? It is when you see everything; it can be a stick standing in ground, a ribbon on a tree branch, or the attitude of the local population. The world is always going to change, and the first step is figuring out what is changing. Then you can determine if you are in danger now because of it.

While I was the Husky driver, only one IED hit a vehicle in our convoy, and that was my vehicle. That day I called an "all stop," so that the convoy wouldn't bunch up. I saw a stick about eighteen inches long stuck into the ground. This was the aiming device. A little further up the road, I noticed a slight change in the color of the dirt. At this point I knew that there was an IED in the road, but I couldn't identify where it was exactly. In order to call up an IED, you must have Positive Identification (PID). "IED" itself is a very broad term and explosives are very complex, so I had to dig the dirt away to find out what this one was made of. My truck had a fifteen-foot mechanical arm attached to the front bumper for just such a situation. I used this to first scrape for wires and then later to dig dirt around where I thought the IED was located. I started to scrape for wires, but then I wanted to get a better position just in case it went off. Just as I stowed my arm and started to move, my little world exploded into a hail of dirt and debris.

It felt similar to falling down a flight of stairs. I could only hear ringing. I felt the *wong, wong, wong* of a concussion as I opened my eyes. I looked from right to left, and all I could see was a cloud of smoke and dust. My training kicked in. There is a drill we were taught to do if we were alone to make sure we weren't hurt. I started at my head and rubbed it, then I looked at my hands to check for blood. I rubbed each arm—still no blood—then my chest, and then down each leg. Once I realized that I didn't die in the explosion, I had to make sure I didn't suffer an injury that would kill me soon after. Physically, I suffered a concussion from the blast, and I was never the same after it. Before that attack, I had no fear of death. I was amazing at my job, and I knew I was better and smarter than my enemy. From that point on, however, I continued to do my job, but the level of terror I felt every time I had to clear another potential IED got worse and worse, even though I knew that the explosion I survived was just bad luck.

That fear spread to almost every aspect of my life. This wasn't necessarily a bad thing, though. I was aware of everything—always on edge, always on lookout. This was a great quality for me as a combat engineer, but it is God-awful for me as a civilian.

As the deployment carried on, I asked to switch jobs from time to time. My platoon leader thought this was a smart idea, and I became a gunner when I was not driving the Husky. Now I was the tough son-of-a-bitch behind a Ma Deuce. Trust me, you do not want to be on the receiving end of this thing. The Ma Deuce is the Browning M2 .50 caliber machine gun.

When I fired that beast, the fear that I felt disappeared, if only for a brief period of time. I only personally, directly engaged the enemy a handful of times. Each time I felt better, maybe because I was making someone else feel as terrified as I usually felt. Anyone who fought in Iraq, if he is honest, will likely admit that he enjoyed that aspect of the war. As Philip Caputo wrote after the war in Vietnam, "It was a peculiar enjoyment because it was mixed with a commensurate pain. Under fire, a man's powers of life heightened in proportion to the proximity of death, so that he felt an elation as extreme as his dread."

My contract came to an end five months before we were scheduled to come home. I was tagged stop-loss, which meant they weren't sending me home when I was supposed to go. All I wanted to do was go home and put this God-forsaken year behind me. While we were getting ready to leave the country, our retention NCO asked me if I wanted to reenlist. I decided that I did want to stay in because of what I had to offer to all the other junior enlisted members. I thought I had some great skills and experiences that I could pass on to them. I signed on for another three years and passed on as much knowledge as I possibly could before leaving.

Deciding to leave the Army left me with the same feelings as I had when I thought about all the difficult decisions I made during my deployment: hate, frustration, anger, and guilt. I deal with all of these things to this day. I hated that I had to become angry, violent, and dangerous to survive. I was frustrated and angry that I had become so terrified of being blown up. And I felt guilty that the only thing that made me feel better was to make someone else feel terrified to die. When I first got out, I tried to numb these emotions—my depression—with alcohol. Eventually, I decided to kill myself.

I came home one day after a really shitty day of arguing with my brother. On my way home, some asshole cut me off. I know these are relatively small issues, but I just couldn't deal with any of it anymore. I just wanted everything to stop. I pulled into my driveway and drove straight into the garage. I sat there for a minute contemplating what I was about to do. I clicked the button, and the overhead door shut behind me. I was sad and happy at the same time. As the car continued to fill the garage with exhaust, I thought about everyone I had ever met and how this decision would impact them. In that moment, the lowest point of my life, I realized that one choice—my choice—could have such a huge impact.

Despite all I had been through, all I had endured, I remembered that I still have the ability to make a profound impact on my life and in the lives of those around me. Once I realized that, I turned the car off and called the suicide hotline. I took the first steps in my new life, away from the crazy bullshit that had entangled me for so long. This has not been an easy road to take, and every day since has been a challenge, but I'm in college now working on that degree I wanted before the Army. Was the Army the best path for me? I like to think that I came out with more than I went in with. I have some of my greatest memories while serving in the Army, but I also have some of my worst. As I stand today, I have a bright future ahead of me, so I'm not going to dwell on the things I can't change. Instead, I'm going to focus on what I can.

AFTERWORD

By Matthew J. Hefti

"Then you find yourself standing outside yourself."
—Tyler Pozolinski, "Not Everyone
Who Comes Home Is Home"

I'm wholly unqualified to be writing this afterword. You see, I'm still dealing with my own reprogramming and assimilation after leaving the military less than a year prior to this writing. Perhaps I didn't fully understand that when I agreed to participate in this project. If you've made it to this point, you probably already realize that this compendium isn't the literary masterpiece usually praised with Pulitzers and National Book Awards. These are not necessarily the most intellectual essays in the world. *See Me for Who I Am* is, however, the most real thing I've read all year. It is also one of the most important collections of essays I've read all year.

The young people who poured their hearts into the essays in this book are still in the most nascent stages of their liberal arts education. The authors—with limited exceptions—engage in no literary reflection; they do not deconstruct thematic threads, nor do they make an effort to place their work within the larger historical or literary context of the current canon of emerging war literature. I still feel compelled, however, to explain the perspective of this work, to contextualize it, to frame these essays in a way that demonstrates some genius subtext, visible only upon close inspection and explication.

Fortunately, no such complex analysis exists. Each individual essay here resists contextualization. No individual essay can serve as a stand-in for the rest of the military or for the experiences of all veterans. The essays are not filtered through lenses of Marxism, Narratology, Feminism, Modernism, Post-Modernism, Structuralism, or Psychoanalytic Criticism. The only filter for these essays is the raw, gritty lens of experience.

Therein lies the true value of these essays. The uncultivated nature of this book is exactly what makes it required reading; that rawness is what sets this book apart from others on the same topic. These college freshmen—often older and worldlier than their peers—are walking straight off the battlefield with the dust still trailing off their boots, the blood still speckling their uniforms, and the gun smoke still stinging their nostrils. There is no irony here; *See Me for Who I Am* is real talk.

David Chrisinger has done far more here than create a short book of essays; he has demonstrated to an entire group of young veterans that—whether they recognized it as they were writing their essays or not—they can still work as a team and accomplish great things, even after taking off the uniform. Whether this important group of essays sells one hundred copies or 10,000 copies, the names of these young veterans are now indelibly etched together as a unit—as the contributors to this book, *See Me for Who I Am*—in the relative immortality of a published piece of literature. That is no small thing. For what it's worth, I couldn't be prouder to have my name in the same book as theirs.

Yet, it's so much more important than that, because isn't that sense of cohesiveness—the nature of being part of a team working toward something common and greater than ourselves—isn't the camaraderie what we miss the most? It isn't that any single one of us misses starving on the side of a mountain as we hump our packs, explosives, and weapons on a mission from which we may not return. It's not that any one of us misses waking up before the sun shines her face and then not quitting until she begins to rise for the second time since we started. It's not that any one of us misses months and years away from our families, hometowns, or loved ones.

But we do all miss each other.

I propose that what we miss the most is not the thrill of war, but the satisfaction that comes from subjecting our individual wills to the common good—the satisfaction that comes from putting the group first, no matter the cost to our individual selves. That is what we miss. We don't necessarily miss the military life; we miss the military way of life; in other words, we miss a way of life in which we all work together. We miss a way of life in which it is taken for granted that we are all stronger when we are together. We miss a way of life in which we all understand we're on the same team.

And that's why this book is so important. For the writers. For the veterans who read it. For the civilians who read it. Chrisinger has shown that even when we think we're struggling, our collective struggles in the aggregate demonstrate to each and every one of us that we are not alone. I am not alone. You are not alone. And that is no small thing.

That realization—that ability to stand outside ourselves to look at ourselves, to see that our humanity extends far beyond our individuality, to see that it touches everyone with whom we come in contact—well, that's when we start our journey home. And it's only when we recognize that all those "others" who surround us are members of a team far more valuable than ourselves that any of us really feel at home.

For the civilians trying to understand why veterans think the way they think, for the veterans trying to bridge the military-civilian divide, for the casual reader looking for a nugget of wisdom, for the social justice warrior looking to empathize or connect, for the transitioning Special Operations Forces leader wondering how anything else can measure up, for the veteran trying to learn her place and learn her purpose as she takes off her uniform, for any reader interested in the welfare of her fellow human beings, the simple answer at the front of any question of how to live is a declaration of motivation—a declaration of purpose. Whether we have ever worn a uniform or not, whether we used to wear a uniform or still do, we can still all do great and courageous things for the same reason these brave young warriors did anything of value in our most recent wars: for those on our left and those on our right.

Matthew J. Hefti
June 27, 2015
Madison, Wisconsin

CONTRIBUTING AUTHOR
BIOGRAPHIES

BRIAN CASTNER:

Brian is the author of *The Long Walk* (Doubleday), an Amazon Best Book of 2012. He previously served as an explosive ordnance disposal officer, commanding bomb disposal units in Balad and Kirkuk, Iraq and as a military contractor and consultant, training soldiers and Marines prior to their tours in Iraq and Afghanistan. His journalism, essays, and reviews have appeared at *Wired, The New York Times, Foreign Policy, VICE News, The Los Angeles Review of Books, Outside, The Daily Beast,* and on *National Public Radio.*

CHASE VUCHETICH:

Chase grew up in Park Falls, Wisconsin and joined the United States Marine Corps before he graduated from high school. He served with 1st Battalion, 5th Marines as a 0311 Infantryman and deployed to Sangin, Afghanistan from March through October 2011. He also deployed with the 31st Marine Expeditionary Unit in the Asia-Pacific region. He is now studying athletic training at the University of Wisconsin-Stevens Point.

JOSH THUNDER:

Josh was raised in Wausau, Wisconsin and joined the United States Army in 2010. He served as a 25F Network Switching Systems Operator/Maintainer and was stationed at Fort Sill, Oklahoma with the 31st Air Defense Artillery Brigade. He was deployed to Ali al Salem, Kuwait in October 2012 and served there for a year, mainly providing relay communications for the Patriot Air Defense in Kuwait. He got married in January 2014 and is now studying computer information systems at the University of Wisconsin-Stevens Point.

LEON VALLIERE:

Leon grew up on the Lac du Flambeau Reservation in Wisconsin. He served in the United States Navy and was stationed on Camp H.M. Smith Hawaii. He was a Petty Officer Second Class Information Systems and was the Lead Service Technician for Executive Communications Headquarters U.S. Pacific Command. His is now studying physics at the University of Wisconsin-Stevens Point and wants to eventually become a teacher on a reservation so he can help Native youth.

GEOFFRY NORFLEET:

Geoffry was born and raised in Sulphur Springs, Texas and graduated from high school in Rosholt, Wisconsin. Soon after graduation, he joined the United States Army as an infantryman and was stationed in Vilseck, Germany for three years. He deployed for ten months to Kandahar Province, Afghanistan, just north of the Pakistani border. He left the Army as a specialist and is now studying sports physiology at the University of Wisconsin-Stevens Point. His goal is to one day open his own sports rehabilitation clinic.

SEAN CASEY:

Sean grew up in the small farming town of Loyal, Wisconsin. If you blink while driving through it, he says, you'll probably miss the whole town. Sean joined the United States Marine Corps—"the world's greatest fighting force"—so that he could explore the world outside of Loyal. Sean spent three years in Germany with Marine Forces Europe and Africa Command as an 0111 Administrative Specialist. He says he hit the jackpot with that assignment, and he's not afraid to brag about it. After his brief yet very rewarding military career, he decided to attend the University Wisconsin-Stevens Point so that he could major in Business Administration. When he graduates, he would like to become a business consultant specializing in productivity and performance.

NATHAN COWARD:

Nathan grew up in Sun Prairie, Wisconsin and joined the United States Army in 2000. He served as an 11B Infantryman and was stationed at Fort McNair in Washington, D.C. He was near the Pentagon on 9/11 and spent a month conducting rescue and recovery work there. He was medically retired in 2004 and moved back to Wisconsin. Nathan is currently taking general coursework at the University of Wisconsin-Stevens Point and has not yet decided on a major.

ROSS PETERSEN:

Ross grew up in Luck, Wisconsin and graduated from Luck High School in 2009. Soon after graduation, he joined the United States Marine Corps and served as an Intelligence Analyst for four years. He was stationed in Okinawa, Japan from 2010 to 2012. During that time, he was able to go to Thailand and South Korea. He is currently studying chemistry at the University of Wisconsin-Stevens Point and wants to put that knowledge to good use in the renewable energy sector.

JOHN ELBERT:

John was born in Wausau, Wisconsin and joined the United States Army as an information systems operator. He served overseas on three deployments: one to Iraq and two to Afghanistan. He is currently studying business and economics at the University of Wisconsin-Stevens Point.

YVETTE M. PINO:

Yvette grew up in New Mexico and was living near New York City on September 11, 2001. The attacks that day inspired her to join the United States Army, where she was assigned to the 101st Airborne Division. Yvette deployed to Iraq in support of Operation Iraqi Freedom from 2003 to 2004. While serving in Iraq, Yvette found a sense of solitude in creating works of art, where her art was identified and appreciated by her commanding officers, including General David Petraeus. This earned her the unofficial title of "Division Artist." The title later followed her on her second deployment to Iraq in 2005 to 2006, where she created more works of art, boosting the morale of her fellow troops. Following her active duty service, Yvette served with the 1175th Military Police Battalion, Missouri National Guard, where she was activated to assist with relief efforts during the 2008 Mississippi River floods. After receiving her BFA from the University of Wisconsin-Madison, Yvette founded the Veteran Print Project, which seeks to open an ongoing dialogue between two divergent groups—veterans and artists—to express the historical experiences of veterans through the traditional methods of fine art print.

TRAVIS JOCHIMSEN:

Travis grew up in Medford, Wisconsin and joined the United States Army at age nineteen. The primary occupation he held for the twelve years he served was 92F Petroleum Supply Specialist. Travis was stationed at Fort Carson in Colorado and Fort Knox in Kentucky and deployed to Iraq four times. He is currently studying forestry management at the University of Wisconsin-Stevens Point. He is married and has a two-year-old son, and he looks forward to becoming a certified forester.

RYAN CALLAHAN:

Ryan was born in Giessen, Germany and moved to Watersmeet, Michigan when he was twelve years old. He joined the United States Army as Airborne Infantry at the age of eighteen and was stationed at Joint Base Lewis-McChord in the state of Washington. He deployed to Afghanistan four separate times. He is currently majoring in German, Computer Information Systems, and Web Design and Media Development at the University of Wisconsin-Stevens Point. His favorite hobby is studying martial arts.

MATT FORTUN:

Matt grew up in Viola, Wisconsin and served in the United States Army as a 12Y Geospatial Engineer. He deployed to Mazar-i-Sharif, Afghanistan during the drawdown. He is now studying forestry management at the University of Wisconsin-Stevens Point and enjoys, above all else, anything he can do outside.

TYLER POZOLINSKI:

Tyler grew up in Neenah, Wisconsin and joined the United States Marine Corps in 2010. He served with 1st Battalion, 5th Marines as an 0341 Mortarman. He deployed to Sangin, Afghanistan from March through April 2011. He also deployed with the 31st Marine Expeditionary Unit in the Asia-Pacific region. He left the Marine Corps in June 2014 and is now studying nursing at the University of Wisconsin-Stevens Point.

KYLE NOWAK:

Kyle grew up in Stratford, Wisconsin, where he was a stand-out in multiple varsity sports. He joined the United States Army as an 11B Infantryman and deployed to Kirkuk, Iraq in 2010. He is now studying Clinical Laboratory Science at the University of Wisconsin-Stevens Point, where he is also a member of the varsity men's track and field team.

ZACH TRZINSKI:

Zach grew up in Amherst, Wisconsin and joined the United States Army in 2010. He served with Delta Company 508th Parachute Infantry Regiment, 2nd Battalion, 4th Combat Brigade, 82nd Airborne Division. He served as an 11B M240B Machine Gunner and deployed to Zhari District in Kandahar Province, Afghanistan from February through August 2012. He is currently studying wildland fire science at the University of Wisconsin-Stevens Point and looks forward to fighting forest fires upon graduation.

CODY MAKUSKI:

Cody grew up in Amherst, Wisconsin and joined the United States Army in 2010. He served as a 19D Airborne Cavalry Scout. He was stationed at Fort Bragg in North Carolina for four years and deployed with Bravo Troop 3-73 Cavalry Squadron, 1st Brigade Combat Team, 82nd Airborne Division to Ghazni Province, Afghanistan in 2012. He left the Army in 2014 at the rank of specialist and married his wife, Amanda. They now have a beautiful baby daughter, and Cody is studying forestry management at the University of Wisconsin-Stevens Point. He loves to hunt, fish, camp, and spend time in the outdoors and hopes to one day be able to live happily ever after far away from civilization, with his family in the middle of nowhere.

SARA POQUETTE:

Sara grew up in Madison, Wisconsin and served eleven years as a broadcast journalist in the Wisconsin Army National Guard (WIARNG). Sara completed two year-long deployments: Operation Iraqi Freedom II in 2004 and Cuba in 2008. Before medically separating from the military in 2012 as a staff sergeant, Sara completed her BA in Psychology, completed a year of graduate courses in social work, and held various civilian positions with the WIARNG as Deputy Director of Public Affairs, Yellow Ribbon Reintegration Program Event Coordinator, and Sexual Assault Response Coordinator. Sara moved to Texas in October 2012 and became a Community Relations Manager for Allies in Service—a Dallas nonprofit dedicated to assisting veterans and their spouses. She is very active in Iraq and Afghanistan Veterans of America and currently works as a Digital Communications Specialist at The Center for BrainHealth at the University of Texas at Dallas.

BRETT FOLEY:

Brett grew up in Rhinelander, Wisconsin and joined the United States Marine Corps the summer before he graduated from high school. He served two combat deployments: one to Iraq in 2007 and another to Afghanistan in 2010. In Afghanistan, Brett was a member of a Ground Sensor Platoon in Helmand Province attached to the 1st Battalion, 3rd Marines. Shortly after he left the Marine Corps, Brett began working with David Chrisinger on a campaign to raise awareness of issues affecting post-9/11 veterans. In October 2013, Brett and Chrisinger ran a fifty-mile ultramarathon after raising more than $7,000 for a non-profit organization that helps post-9/11 veterans transition out of the military. After graduating with an AA in criminology from Madison Area Technical College, Brett found a job as a county sheriff deputy in Wisconsin.

ZACHARY RUESCH:

Zachary grew up in Rib Lake, Wisconsin and served in the Wisconsin Army National Guard as a combat engineer for seven years, achieving the rank of sergeant. His unit—the 951st Engineer Company, Sapper—was based out of Rhinelander and Tomahawk, Wisconsin and was deployed to Afghanistan in 2009 to conduct route clearance missions. He saw much of the country, including Paktika, Ghazni, Zabul, Kandahar, Kabul, Logar, and Wardak. Upon his return, he began studying history and broad-field social science at the University of Wisconsin-Stevens Point. While Zachary never took David Chrisinger's freshman seminar, he was instrumental in helping develop the course. Since graduating from college, Zachary has taught in a number of school districts around Wisconsin, "corrupting future generations," he says. He is currently teaching sociology and psychology in the Omro School District. Zachary hopes that sharing his experiences and perspectives will help others accept, adjust, and accomplish. He also wishes to thank the people and relationships that have helped give his life true meaning and purpose: Jacqueline, Rynn, Lincoln, and Quinn.

AARON LEWIS:

Aaron grew up in Mosinee, Wisconsin, where he was the middle child in a large family of seven. At the age of twenty-one, Aaron joined the United States Army and became an engineer stationed out of Fort Carson, Colorado. He was deployed from 2009 to 2010 in support of Operation Iraqi Freedom and Operation Enduring Freedom. Aaron was discharged from the military in 2011 and is currently attending the University of Wisconsin-Stevens Point, where he is double-majoring in Accounting and Business Management. After graduation, Aaron is planning to become a licensed certified public accountant.

MATTHEW J. HEFTI:

Matthew is the author of *A Hard and Heavy Thing* (Tyrus Books/F+W, January 2016). He was born in Canada and grew up in Wisconsin. After 9/11, he visited the Armed Forces recruiter. He then spent twelve years as an explosive ordnance disposal technician. He deployed twice to Iraq and twice to Afghanistan, spending one tour in Iraq as an EOD team member and the remaining three tours as an EOD team leader. While enlisted, he earned a BA in English and an MFA in Creative Writing. His words have been seen in—among others—War, Literature & the Arts; Blue Moon Literary & Art Review; and Chad Harbach's MFA vs. NYC. He is now working, studying, and living in Madison, Wisconsin, where he is pursuing his JD at the

University of Wisconsin Law School. He and his lovely wife have three pretty neat daughters, who keep them from taking themselves too seriously.

ACKNOWLEDGMENTS

This book wouldn't exist were it not for Brett Foley and his wife, Whitney. In high school, Brett and I were pretty lousy baseball players, so we spent most of our time on the bench, talking about life and all the other things fifteen-year-old boys worry about. Perhaps I shouldn't be so surprised, then, that Brett opened up to me after he returned home from his second combat deployment. Much of my class at the University of Wisconsin-Stevens Point and the idea for this book grew from those conversations. He opened my eyes to something that was hiding in plain sight. He forever altered the course of my life in profoundly positive ways. He helped me make sense of what my grandfather had experienced during the Second World War, and he helped bring closure not only to me, but to my father's entire family.

The class that produced these essays would not have been possible without the tireless help and sage wisdom of Nancy LoPatin-Lummis. When I was a young undergraduate student, Nancy saw something in me, and ever since then, she hasn't stopped helping. Not only did she mentor me throughout my undergraduate career, but she has also supported (and sometimes defended) me in a variety of ways in nearly every endeavor I have undertaken. I can say quite honestly that I wouldn't be where I am today without her. I also wish to personally thank the following people at the University of Wisconsin-Stevens Point for their mentorship, enthusiasm, kindness, and continued support: Ann Whipp, Tom Wetter, Bob Erickson, Valerie Barske, Lee Willis, Tim Krause, Nick Schultz, Dan Kellogg, Ron Strege, Ed Lee, Todd Huspeni, Greg Summers, Chris Cirmo, Al Thompson, and Bernie Patterson. Each of them saw the value in what we are trying to accomplish and have stopped at nothing to help us continue.

A special thank you goes out to Yvette M. Pino, my friend and the founder of The Veteran Print Project. She and I collaborated during the spring semester of 2015 with an art professor on campus, Bob Erickson, to bring together my veteran students—some of whom contributed to this collection—with Bob's printmaking students. Yvette's project is simple yet powerful. My students shared their stories of military service with Bob's students, and then those students created fine art prints illustrating what they had learned. I believe Tolstoy said it best: the purpose of art is to provide a bridge of empathy between the artist and others. That is exactly what The Veteran Print Project is all about. I wish every veteran could feel what it's like to have their stories and experiences not only validated, but also enshrined in a beautiful piece of artwork.

In addition, I'd like to thank each of the veterans who contributed to this collection for opening up their lives to me. I can say without equivocation that my students are some of the best people I've ever had the privilege to know. I feel honored and humbled to have been welcomed along on their long journeys home from war.

This project wouldn't have become what it has without the encouragement and support of Brian Castner. I discovered Brian's book in a kiosk at the airport in Seattle. From the moment I began reading, I knew he was a special kind of writer. His honesty was so refreshing and went a long way toward helping me understand what our veterans experience when they return from war. When I decided to send him an email out of the blue almost two years ago, I had no idea that he would write me back that same day, ready to offer any assistance I needed. That's the kind of guy he is. All the good things that are happening to him are well-deserved.

I'd also like to acknowledge the incredible vision and tireless effort put forth by my publisher, Sue Petrie. From the very first time we spoke, I knew she was the right person to shepherd this project along. It has been such an honor to work with someone who cares as much about these students and their stories as I do.

I'd like to end by thanking my family. To my father, for opening himself up to me and helping me make sense of my family's hidden past. To my mother, for always being there to listen to my ideas and offer a few of her own. Their love and support has proven invaluable to me. Lastly, and most importantly, I'd like to thank my beautiful wife, Ashley, for her never-failing sympathy, understanding, and encouragement.

THE VETERAN PRINT PROJECT

In the spring semester of 2015, some of the students whose essays are featured in this collection told their stories to advanced printmaking students at the University of Wisconsin-Stevens Point in collaboration with The Veteran Print Project. An Iraq War veteran named Yvette M. Pino founded The Veteran Print Project in 2009, and its mission is simple yet powerful: (1) To obtain and develop oral histories of a new generation of veterans, and (2) to connect local artists with the veterans to create fine art prints based on the oral histories.

Tolstoy said that the purpose of art was to provide a bridge of empathy between the artist and others. We took that concept one step further. By sharing their stories, my students connected with their artists, eliciting empathy and a better sense of understanding. The artists then illustrated what they discovered for you, the viewer. The veterans then had the amazing opportunity to bear witness to their own stories and to see the ways in which their illustrated stories affected other viewers.

It is my hope that the essays and prints you find in this collection will transform the way you think about war and those who serve our country. I know it has for me.

Print by Emily Sikora, inspired by Tyler Pozolinski.

David Chrisinger is an Associate Lecturer at the University of Wisconsin-Stevens Point, where he teaches a veteran re-integration course to new student veterans. He is also the Founder and Managing Editor of *Stronger at the Broken Places,* a website dedicated not only to raising awareness of the struggles and triumphs of American veterans throughout history, but also to helping today's generation of student veterans tell their stories of war and coming home.

ABOUT HUDSON WHITMAN

Hudson Whitman is a small press affiliated with Excelsior College in upstate New York.

Our tagline is "Books That Make a Difference," and we aim to publish high-quality nonfiction books and multimedia projects in areas that complement Excelsior's academic strengths: education, nursing, health care, military interests, business and technology, with one "open" category, American culture and society.

If you would like to submit a manuscript or proposal, please review the guidelines on our website, hudsonwhitman.com. Feel free to send a note with any questions. We endeavor to respond as soon as possible.

OTHER TITLES BY HUDSON WHITMAN

The Language of Men: A Memoir
by Anthony D'Aries

Shot: Staying Alive with Diabetes
by Amy F. Ryan

The Sanctuary of Illness: A Memoir of Heart Disease
by Thomas Larson

*The Call of Nursing: Stories from the Front Lines
of Health Care* by William Patrick

*Courageous Learning:
Finding a New Path through Higher Education*
by John Ebersole, with William Patrick